JOHN LE NEVE

Fasti Ecclesiae Anglicanae

1300–1541

JOHN LE NEVE

Fasti Ecclesiae Anglicanae
1300-1541

XI
The Welsh Dioceses
(Bangor, Llandaff, St Asaph, St Davids)

COMPILED BY B. JONES

UNIVERSITY OF LONDON
INSTITUTE OF HISTORICAL RESEARCH
THE ATHLONE PRESS
1965

Published by
THE ATHLONE PRESS
UNIVERSITY OF LONDON
at 2 Gower Street, London WC1
Distributed by Constable & Co Ltd
12 Orange Street, London WC2

Canada
Oxford University Press
Toronto

U.S.A.
Oxford University Press Inc
New York

© *University of London,* 1965

Printed in Great Britain by
WESTERN PRINTING SERVICES LTD
BRISTOL

Foreword

THE scarcity of Welsh ecclesiastical records for the period 1300–1541 has been a serious handicap to the compilation of this volume and accounts for the many gaps in the lists of cathedral dignitaries. In Llandaff diocese the bishops' registers and cathedral chapter acts begin in 1660, St Asaph diocese has some fragments of six-teenth-century material, in Bangor diocese the register of Benedict Nicholls has sur-vived for the fifteenth century and there are some thin sixteenth-century registers. St Davids diocese has the register of Guy de Mona and part of that of Henry Chichele for the early years of the fifteenth century, and the registers of Richard Martin, Huw Pavy and Edward Fychan, which cover the years 1482–1483, 1485–1496 and 1509–1523, but four other registers have been lost since the eighteenth century when Edward Yardley, archdeacon of Cardigan 1739–c. 1770, compiled his book *Menevia Sacra*. For this work he used the registers of Benedict Nicholls and Thomas Rodburn, 1417–1442, which do not appear to have been seen since his time, and additional volumes of the registers of Henry Chichele and John Hiot, vicar general of St Davids, of the early fifteenth century. Edward Yardley was unusual among antiquarians of his day in that, in most cases, he gave clear references to the folios of the registers which he used, and not the usual vague references to 'an old manuscript which I have seen' or to 'Reg. Cantuar'', which are so familiar in the works of some of his contemporaries. Attempt has been made to trace the descendants of Edward Yardley in case the lost registers should be lying about in some forgotten place, but all research of this nature has proved fruitless. Directions given in his will about the disposal of his library were vague: 'Item as to my library either of manuscripts or printed books my mind and will is that if I shall leave behinde me any directions bearing date after this my will and signed with my hand, such directions shall be pursued and followed and that my executors shall be pleased to see them disposed of according to my intention signified thereby' (PCC 30 Jenner). Yardley's library was sold at Sotheby's sale rooms in October 1800 but there is no mention of the registers of St Davids among his manu-scripts listed in the sale catalogue. Edward Yardley had few relatives at the time of his death, and the greater part of his money was left to the Society for the Promotion of Christian Knowledge. Work has been done on the archives of this society where there is a lot of information about this aspect of Edward Yardley's career, but no further information about the registers of St Davids has emerged.

A miscellaneous variety of material has been used for the Welsh volume of the *Fasti* and it has been necessary to search all the English episcopal registers in the hope of finding exchanges of benefices between English and Welsh clergy. Information has come from almost every English diocese, even from York and Durham in the northern province. The papal registers have not been of as much assistance for the Welsh volume as they have been for the other volumes of the *Fasti*, because, probably owing to the poverty of the Welsh dioceses, only one cardinal held office in Wales during the entire period 1300–1541—Louis Donati, cardinal priest of S. Marcus, who was provided to the 'golden prebend', Mathry, in St Davids, and held it for a few years during the late fourteenth century. In addition to the prebendaries of the four dioceses, canons have been included, as it may subsequently be possible to discover which prebend they held. Bangor cathedral had only two prebends, but a number of persons called 'canons' of Bangor have been found. The two terms, canon and prebendary, appear to have often been used synonymously by contemporary scribes, but in this volume, as far as possible, separate lists have been made; first of prebendaries holding named prebends, secondly of unidentified prebendaries, then of persons holding a canonry with expectation of a prebend in the future, and lastly of persons who occur only as canons. The St Davids list has the further addition of the cursal prebendaries, who are listed before the unidentified prebendaries.[1]

Personal names have been rendered as far as possible in their Welsh forms: e.g. Vaughan appears as Fychan, Trevaur as Trefor, Griffiths as Gruffudd and Howell as Hywel, etc. Although several of these names appear in anglicised forms in other volumes of the *Fasti*, e.g. John Trefor as John Trevaur in *Hereford*, etc., Edward Fychan as Vaughan in *St Paul's, London*, etc., it is considered that the consolidated index of the volumes for the period 1300 to 1541 will bring together those persons whose names appear in both English and Welsh. Powell, Price, Bowen and similar names have been given in their older Welsh forms as ap Hywel, ap Rhys, ab Owain, etc. The Christian names Hugh and David have been given in both Welsh and English forms, because an attempt has been made to distinguish between Welshmen and Englishmen: e.g. Dafydd ap Gruffudd, Dafydd ab Ieuan ab Iorwerth, but David Stedman, David Oliver. When David occurs as a surname a similar distinction has been made, viz. Dafydd Fychan ap Dafydd, and Madog ap Dafydd Llwyd, but John David and Thomas David. No alteration has been made of the surname Davy. Similarly the name Hugh has been given as Huw when the rest of the name denotes an obvious Welshman: viz. Huw ab Owain, Huw Goch, Huw Morgan etc. but Hugh Alcock, Hugh Cotyngham, Hugh de Welhampton etc. In some cases it is impossible to tell whether a person was Welsh or English and here preference has been given to the English form of the name. For example, although Hugh le Yonge was probably Welsh (Young or Younger =Fychan), he is given here as Hugh and not Huw, as the English form of his surname is used in all sources. David Barret could have been Welsh, of Barry, and similarly David Nuporte and David Newcastle, who occur in Llandaff diocese, were probably local men, of Newport,[2] and of Newcastle,[3] but as there is insufficient evidence to prove their Welsh nationality, David has been given in the English form. All Christian names followed immediately by ap or ab are to be found indexed under the initial letter of the Christian name; e.g. the name Llywellyn ap Madog ab Elis will be found under L, not M or E.

Place names have been taken, as in the other volumes of the *Fasti*, from *The Survey Gazetteer of the British Isles*, ed. J. Bartholomew (9th ed., Edinburgh, 1950) and the names of the Welsh cathedral prebends from the appropriate diocesan handbooks or from the 1963 edition of Crockford's *Clerical Directory*. In the index, the Welsh forms

---

[1] For further discussion of the order of the dignitaries, see Appendix, p. 86.

[2] There are two Newports in Wales alone—Pemb. and Mon., and twenty-two other Newports are listed in *The Survey Gazetteer of the British Isles*, ed. J. Bartholomew (9th ed. Edinburgh, 1950).

[3] There are four Newcastles in Wales and the border counties: Newcastle, Mon., Newcastle, Radnor., Newcastle, nr. Clun, Salop, Newcastle, Glam., and also Newcastle Emlyn, Carm., Newcastle Higher, Glam., and several English Newcastles. The difficulty of identifying surnames with place names is shown by these examples.

of place names have been inserted in brackets after the standard form recognised in the British Isles and have been taken from *A Gazetteer of Welsh Place Names*, ed. Elwyn Davies (Cardiff, 1957). It has been felt that to give the Welsh form of the place names would narrow the utility of the book considerably, as many of the correct Welsh names are not widely known even in Wales itself and do not yet appear on the Ordnance Survey maps of the areas; e.g. Lampeter is more familiar even in Cardiganshire than Llanbedr pont Steffan, and the name Brecon more widely known than Aber Honddu. As the names of Italian places in the other volumes have been put into English, and Florence and Venice etc. given instead of the Italian form, the same method has been used for Wales.

I should like to thank Professor Sir Goronwy Edwards and Professor Glanmor Williams for their help in reading the typescript of this volume and for their constructive suggestions for its improvement, and Mr. Milwyn Griffiths of the National Library of Wales, Aberystwyth, for his help with the identification of several Welsh place names.

B.J.

Contents

References

WORKS IN PRINT

Antiquitates Parochiales. — 'Antiquitates Parochiales', by H. Rowlands in *Archaeologia Cambrensis*, series I, vol. I, 1846.

Black Prince's Reg. — *Register of Edward the Black Prince preserved in the Public Record Office.* 4 vols. London, 1930–3.

Brut y Tywysogyon. — *Brut y Tywysogyon or The Chronicle of the Princes Peniarth MS. 20 version*, ed. T. Jones (Board of Celtic Studies, University of Wales, History and Law series, no. xi). Cardiff, 1952.

CCR. — *Calendar of the Close Rolls preserved in the Public Record Office.* 54 vols. London, 1892–1954.

CPL. — *Calendar of Entries in the Papal Registers relating to Great Britain and Ireland: Papal letters.* 14 vols. in 15. London, 1893–1960.

CPP. — *Calendar of Entries in the Papal Registers relating to Great Britain and Ireland: Petitions to the Pope, 1342–1419*, vol. I. London, 1896.

CPR. — *Calendar of the Patent Rolls preserved in the Public Record Office.* London, 1891–1916.

Cal. Anct. Correspondence. — *Calendar of Ancient Correspondence concerning Wales*, by J. G. Edwards (Board of Celtic Studies, University of Wales, History and Law series, no. ii). Cardiff, 1935.

Cartae et Munimenta de Glamorgan. — *Cartae et alia Munimenta quae ad Dominium de Glamorgancia pertinent*, comp. G. T. Clark, ed. G. L. Clark. 6 vols. Cardiff, 1910.

Cat. Anct. Deeds. — *Descriptive Catalogue of Ancient Deeds in the Public Record Office.* 6 vols. London, 1890–1915.

Emden, Reg. Camb. — *Biographical Register of the University of Cambridge to 1500*, comp. A. B. Emden. Cambridge, 1963.

Emden, Reg. Ox. — *Biographical Register of the University of Oxford to 1500*, comp. A. B. Emden. 3 vols. Oxford, 1957–9.

Eubel. — *Hierarchia Catholica Medii Aevi*, ed. C. Eubel. 3 vols. Münster, 1913–23.

Foedera. — *Foedera, conventiones, literae et cujuscunque generis acta publica inter reges Angliae et alios imperatores*, ed. T. Rymer. 10 vols. 3rd edition, 1745.

L. & P. — *Letters and Papers of the Reign of Henry VIII*, ed. J. S. Brewer. London, 1862–1932.

Memorials of Llandaff. *Memorials of the See and Cathedral of Llandaff,* by W. de Gray Birch. Neath, 1912.

Menevia Sacra. *Menevia Sacra,* by Edward Yardley . . . archdeacon of Cardigan 1739–1770, ed. F. Green. Cambrian Archaeological Association, supplemental vol. London, 1927.

R.S.A. *Registrum Sacrum Anglicanum,* by W. Stubbs. Oxford, 1897.

Reg. Bourgchier. *Registrum Thome Bourgchier, Cantuariensis archiepiscopi, 1454–1486,* ed. F. R. H. Du Boulay. Canterbury and York Society, liv, 1957.

Reg. Chichele. *The Register of Henry Chichele, archbishop of Canterbury, 1414–1443,* ed. E. F. Jacob. 4 vols. Canterbury and York Society, xlii, xlv–xlvii, 1937–47.

Reg. Corbridge. *The Register of Thomas of Corbridge, lord archbishop of York, 1300–1304,* ed. W. Brown. 2 vols. Surtees Society, cxxxviii, cxli, 1925–8.

Reg. Langham. *Registrum Simonis Langham, Cantuariensis archiepiscopi,* ed. A. C. Wood. Canterbury and York Society, liii, 1956.

Reg. Nicholls. 'The register of Benedict, bishop of Bangor, 1408–1417', transcribed by A. I. Pryce in *Archaeologia Cambrensis,* lxxvii (1922), 80–107.

Reg. Patrington. 'A fragment of the register of Stephen Patryngton, bishop of St Davids', ed. H. D. Emanuel in *Journal of the Historical Society of the Church in Wales,* ii (1950), 31–45.

Reg. St Davids. *The Episcopal Registers of the Diocese of St David's, 1397 to 1518,* ed. R. F. Isaacson. 1 vol. in 2. Cymmrodorion Record Series, no. 6. London, 1917.

Reg. Sudbury. *Registrum Simonis de Sudbiria, diocesis Londoniensis, 1362–1375,* ed. R. C. Fowler. 2 vols. Canterbury and York Society, xxxiv, xxxviii, 1927–38.

Reg. Trefnant. *Registrum Johannis Trefnant, episcopi Herefordensis, 1389–1404,* ed. W. W. Capes. Canterbury and York Society, xx, 1916.

Reg. Winchelsey. *Registrum Roberti Winchelsey, Cantuariensis archiepiscopi, 1294–1313,* ed. Rose Graham. 1 vol. in 2. Canterbury and York Society, li, lii, 1952–6.

Rot. Parl. *Rotuli Parliamentorum.* 6 vols. London, 1783.

Thomas. *History of the Diocese of St Asaph,* by D. R. Thomas. 2nd edition. 3 vols. Oswestry, 1908–13.

Valor. *Valor Ecclesiasticus temp. Henr. VIII.* 6 vols. 1810–25.

Williams. *The Welsh Church from Conquest to Reformation,* by Glanmor Williams. Cardiff, 1962.

Abbreviations

The following abbreviations are given in lower case or in capitals as required

abp. archbishop
Add. Additional
adm. admission, admit, admitted
archdcn. archdeacon
archdcnry archdeaconry
B.A. bachelor of arts
B.C.L. bachelor of civil law
B.Cn.L. bachelor of canon law
B.M. bachelor of medicine
B.Th. bachelor of theology
bp. bishop
bpc. bishopric
Brit. Mus. British Museum
c. *circa*
can. canon
card. cardinal
cath. cathedral
certif. certificate
ch. church
chap. chapel
chapt. chapter
coll. collation, collated
colleg. collegiate
conf. confirmation, confirmed
cons. consecration, consecrated
d. death, died
D.C.L. doctor of civil law
depriv. deprived
dioc. diocese
dn. dean
ed. edition, edited by
el. election, elect, elected
exch. exchange, exchanged
f. folio
gr. grant, granted
judgt. judgment
k. king
Lamb. Lambeth
libr. library

lic. licence
lic. *alibi cons.* licence *alibi consecrari*
Lic.C.L. licentiate of civil law
lic. el. licence to elect
M. *magister*, master
mand. mandate
mand. adm. mandate to admit
n.d. no date
Nat. national
O.Can.S.A. order of Augustinian canons
O.Carm. order of Carmelites
O.Carth. order of Carthusians
O.Cist. order of Cistercians
O.Clun. order of Cluniacs
O.F.M. order of Friars Minor
O.F.S.A. order of Friars of St Augustine—
    Austin Friars
O.Gilb. order of Gilbertines
O.P. order of Preachers
O.Prem. order of Premonstratensian
    canons
O.S.B. order of St Benedict
occ. occurrence, occurs
P.R.O. Public Record Office
pr. priest
preb. prebendary, prebend
prov. provision, provided
R.S. Rolls Series
ratif. ratified
reg. register
res. resignation, resigned
reservn. reservation
s.d. same day
Salis. Salisbury
Sch.C.L. scholar of civil law
spir. spiritualities
temps. temporalities
trans. translation, translated
vac. vacancy, vacant, vacated

Bangor 1300-1541

MANUSCRIPT MATERIAL

National Library of Wales, Aberystwyth

B/BR/1. Fragment of the register of bp. Skevington, 1509–33.
B/BR/2. Fragments of the registers of bps. Bulkeley and Bayley, 1541–1631.

Canterbury Cathedral Library

Registers A, Q, S, T.

Lambeth Palace Library

The registers of the archbishops of Canterbury from Reynolds to Cranmer, 1314–1555.

Somerset House

PCC: Registers of wills proved in the prerogative court of Canterbury.

Einion 1267–1307.

Royal assent to el. 12 Dec. 1267 (*CPR. 1266–1272* p. 173). Cons. at Canterbury 1267[1] (Cant., Reg. A f. 307/251). Temps. 5 Jan. 1268 (*CPR. 1266–1272* p. 178). D. before 12 Jan. 1307 (Cant., Reg. A f. 82b/75b).

Gruffudd ab Iorwerth 1307–1309.

Royal petition for lic. *alibi cons.* 12 Jan. 1307, because bp. el. old and infirm (Cant., Reg. A f. 82b/75b). Cons. 26 March at Carlisle, Cumb. (*ibid.* f. 307/251). D. 27 Apr. 1309 (P.R.O., C 84/16/21).

M. Einion Sais 1309–1328.

Lic. el. sought 2 May 1309 (P.R.O., C 84/16/21). Royal assent sought 18 June (P.R.O., C 84/16/24), gr. 5 Aug. (*CPR. 1307–1313* p. 181). Temps. 7 Sept. (*ibid.* p. 188). Conf. by abp. 18 Sept. (*Reg. Winchelsey* II 1109). Cons. 9 Nov. by abp. at Canterbury (*ibid.* pp. 1113–14). D. 26 Jan. 1328 (Cant., Reg. Q f. 172).

M. Matthew de Englefeld 1328–1357.

Lic. el. gr. 13 Feb. 1328 (*CPR. 1327–1330* p. 233). El. 26 Feb. (Cant., Reg. Q ff. 172–173). Royal assent 23 March (*CPR. 1327–1330* p. 253). Cons. 12 June at Canterbury by abp. (Cant., Reg. A ff. 307/251–307b/251b). D. before 15 Apr. 1357 (Lamb., Reg. Islip f. 342b).

[M. Ithel ap Robert B.C.L. 1357.]
M. Thomas de Ringstede O.P., D.Th. 1357–1366.

Ithel ap Robert el. by chapt. at Bangor Aug. 1357 (*CPP.* I 300–1). El. set aside by prov. of Ringstede 21 Aug. (*CPL.* III 581). Lic. *alibi cons.* 17 Sept. (*ibid.* p. 584). Cons. at Avignon 1357 (*R.S.A.*). Spir. 15 Nov. (Lamb., Reg. Islip f. 218b). D. 8 Jan. 1366 (*ibid.* f. 245b).

[Alexander Dalby 1366.]
M. Gervase de Castro O.P., D.Th. 1366–1370.

Dalby nominated by Black Prince n.d. (*CPL.* IV 25). Papal mand. 29 Apr. 1366 to abp. of Bordeaux, France, that he should hold an inquiry and notify the pope within two months whether Dalby understood Welsh well enough to preach in language (*ibid.*). Castro prov. 11 Dec. (*Reg. Langham* pp. 240–1). Spir. 16 Feb. 1367 (*ibid.* pp. 241–2). Cons. n.d. at Avignon (*R.S.A.*). Profession to abp. 6 Nov. (*Reg. Langham* p. 265). D. 24 Sept./30 Oct. 1370 (Lamb., Reg. Wittlesey ff. 117–117b).

Hywel ap Goronwy 1371–1372.

El. by chapt. at Bangor n.d., but el. annulled by pope (Lamb., Reg. Wittlesey ff. 136b–137). Prov. 21 Apr. 1371 (*ibid.*). Cons. n.d. at Avignon (*R.S.A.*). Spir. 31 July (Lamb., Reg. Wittlesey f. 137). D. before 3 Feb. 1372 (*ibid.* ff. 137–137b).

M. John Gilbert O.P., B.Th. 1372–1375.

Prov. 17 March 1372 (Lamb., Reg. Wittlesey ff. 137–137b). Cons. n.d. at Avignon

---

[1] i.e. during the year ending 25 March 1268.

(*R.S.A.*). Temps. 30 Apr. (*Foedera* IV i 214). Spir. 16 July (Lamb., Reg. Wittlesey f. 137b). Profession to abp. 13 Nov. (*ibid.* f. 58). Trans. to Hereford 12 Sept. 1375.

[M. Geoffrey Herdeby O.F.S.A., M.Th.]
M. John Swaffham O.Carm., D.Th. 1376–1398.

Petition to pope n.d. for prov. of Herdeby as bp. (*Cal. Anct. Correspondence* p. 196). Swaffham trans. from Cloyne, Ireland, 2 July 1376 (Lamb., Reg. Sudbury ff. 19b–20). Profession to abp. 22 Oct. (*ibid.* f. 20). Spir. s.d. (*ibid.*). Temps. 28 Oct. (*CPR. 1374–1377* p. 363). D. before 21 July 1398 (*CPR. 1396–1399* p. 386).

[M. Lewis Aber 1398.]
M. Richard Young Lic.Cn. & C.L. 1398–1404.

Lic. el. gr. 21 July 1398 (*CPR. 1396–1399* p. 386). Aber called bp. el. 21 Aug. (*CPL.* V 99). Young prov. 2 Dec. (*ibid.* p. 187). Custody of temps. gr. 21 Oct. 1399 (*CPR. 1399–1401* p. 31). Prov. 28 Nov. (*Eubel* I 130). Plenary restitution of temps. 20 May 1400 (*CPR. 1399–1401* p. 288). Cons. probably at Rome 1400 (*R.S.A.*). Trans. to Rochester 1404.

[Llywellyn Bifort 1404–1407.]
[M. Griffin le Yonge D.Cn.L. 1407–1414.[1]]
M. Benedict Nicholls B.Cn.L. 1408–1417.

Bifort prov. by pope Boniface IX (d. 1 Oct. 1404), held bpc. for three years then ejected by prov. of Yonge 14 Feb. 1407 (*Eubel* I 130; *CPL.* VI 502–3). Nicholls prov. 18 Apr. 1408 (Lamb., Reg. Arundell I ff. 41b–42). Called bp. el. of Bangor 1 May (*CPL.* VI 137). Temps. 22 July (*CPR. 1405–1408* p. 464). Cons. 6 Aug. (*Reg. Nicholls* p. 85). Spir. 10 Aug. (Lamb., Reg. Arundell I f. 42). Bifort gr. royal pardon 5 June 1409 (*CPR. 1408–1413* p. 82). Yonge had been prov. by pope Benedict XIII and Nicholls by pope Gregory XII, acts of both popes declared void at Council of Pisa by ordinance *Item si alique bulle seu littere*, promulgated 13 June (*CPL.* VI 502–3). Nicholls enthroned at Bangor 12 Oct. (*Reg. Nicholls* p. 82). Yonge prov. to bpc. of Ross, Scotland, by pope Benedict XIII 14 Feb. 1414 (*Eubel* I 446). Prov. to Bangor declared void 28 July (*CPL.* VI 502–3). Mand. for restoration of Bifort s.d. (*ibid.*). Did not obtain bpc. since held by Nicholls until trans. to St Davids 1417.

M. William Barrowe D.Cn.L. 1418–1423.

Prov. 14 Feb. 1418 (*Reg. Chichele* I 42–3). Profession to abp. 16 Apr. (*ibid.* p. 43). Temps. 5 June (*CPR. 1416–1422* p. 167). Cons. after 13 Oct. 1419, probably at Council of Constance (*R.S.A.*). Trans. to Carlisle 1423.

M. John Clederowe D.Cn.L. 1423–1435.

Prov. 19 Apr. 1423 (*Eubel* I 130). Called bp. el. 5 May (*CPL.* VII 256). Profession to abp. 20 March 1425 (*Reg. Chichele* I 90). Spir. s.d. (*ibid.*). Temps. 15 Jan. 1426 (*CPR. 1422–1429* p. 330). D. before 13 Dec. 1435 (*Reg. Chichele* II 532–4).

Thomas Cheriton O.P. 1436–1448.

Prov. 5 March 1436 (*CPL.* VIII 575). Lic. *alibi cons.* 24 Nov. (Cant., Reg. S f. 124b/134b). Profession to abp. 6 Feb. 1437 (*Reg. Chichele* I 121). Temps. 21 Nov. (*CPR. 1436–1441* p. 23). Spir. 26 Nov. (*Reg. Chichele* I 121). D. before 2 Jan. 1448 (Lamb., Reg. Stafford f. 29).

---

[1] Yonge still occ. with the title bp. of Bangor 22 Feb. 1414, although Nicholls had been enthroned 12 Oct. 1409 (*Welsh Records in Paris*, ed. T. Matthews (Carmarthen, 1910) p. 110). Yonge had been chancellor to Owain Glyn Dŵr and was one of his most loyal supporters. He was still working on behalf of Glyn Dŵr in France in 1415 and therefore the reason for his never regaining possession of the bpc. of Bangor is obvious (*Williams* pp. 220, 225).

M. John Stanbury O.Carm., D.Th. 1448–1453.

Custody of temps. gr. 25 Jan. 1448 (*Foedera* v iii 185). Prov. 4 March (*CPL.* x 299). Lic. *alibi cons.* 9 March (*ibid.* p. 335). Profession to abp. 4 May (Lamb., Reg. Stafford f. 29b). Temps. 15 May (*CPR. 1446–1452* p. 161). Second lic. *alibi cons.* 20 June (Cant., Reg. S f. 175b/147b). Cons. by abp. s.d. (*R.S.A.*). Trans. to Hereford 1453.

M. James Blakedon O.P., D.Th. 1453–1464.

Trans. from Achonry, Ireland, 7 Feb. 1453 (*CPL.* x 596). Temps. 25 March (*CPR. 1452–1461* p. 49). Profession to abp. 12 Apr. (Lamb., Reg. Kempe f. 216b). Spir. 14 Apr. (*ibid.* f. 217). D. before 3 Oct. 1464 (*CPR. 1461–1467* p. 357).

M. Richard Edenham O.F.M.,[1] D.Th. 1465–1494.

Prov. 14 Jan. 1465 (*CPL.* XII 432). Lic. *alibi cons.* 8 March (Cant., Reg. S f. 214b). Cons. n.d. in England (*R.S.A.*). D. before 13 Apr. 1494 (*CPR. 1485–1494* p. 461).

Henry Deane O.Can.S.A. 1494–1499/1500.

Custody of temps. gr. 13 Apr. 1494 (*CPR. 1485–1494* p. 461). Prov. 4 July (P.R.O., Papal Bulls 37 (7)). Temps. 6 Oct. 1496 (*CPR. 1494–1509* p. 80). Trans. to Salisbury 1499/1500—Bull of trans. 8 Jan. 1500 (*Eubel* II 253), but had been gr. custody of temps. 7 Dec. 1499 (*CPR. 1494–1509* p. 185).

M. Thomas Pigot O.S.B. 1500–1504.

Prov. 4 May 1500 (*Eubel* II 114). Cons. 1500 (*R.S.A.*). D. 15 Aug. 1504 (Lamb., Reg. Warham II f. 218).

M. John Penny O.Can.S.A., D.C.L. Abbot of Leicester. 1505–1508.

Prov. 30 Aug. 1505 (*Eubel* III 143). Lic. *alibi cons.* s.d. (Cant., Reg. T f. 450). Trans. to Carlisle 1508.

Thomas Skevington O.Cist. Abbot of Beaulieu.[2] 1509–1533.

Prov. 23 Feb. 1509 (Lamb., Reg. Warham I f. 12). Lic. *alibi cons.* 12 June (*ibid.* ff. 12–12b). Cons. at Lambeth 17 June (*ibid.* f. 12b). Spir. 20 June (*ibid.* II f. 255). D. 16/17 Aug. 1533 (*L. & P.* VI No. 1007; Lamb., Reg. Cranmer f. 158b).

M. John Salcote *or* **Capon** O.S.B., D.Th. 1533–1539.

El. 23 Nov. 1533/30 Jan. 1534 (*Reg. Sudbury* I 223; Lamb., Reg. Cranmer f. 158b). Royal assent 11 Apr. (*L. & P.* VI No. 587 (14)). El. conf. by abp. 15 Apr. (Lamb., Reg. Cranmer f. 157). Cons. by abp. at Croydon, Surr., 19 Apr. (*ibid.* ff. 162b–163). Temps. 28 Apr. (*L. & P.* VII No. 589 (11)). Trans. to Salisbury 1539.

M. John Birde O.Carm., D.Th. Bp. of Penrith. 1539–1541.

Lic. el. gr. 23 July 1539 (Lamb., Reg. Cranmer f. 238b). El. 24 July (*ibid.*). Royal assent 26 Aug. and 1 Sept. (*L. & P.* XIV ii Nos. 113 (25) and 264 (2)). Temps. 9 Sept. (*Foedera* VI iii 37). Conf. by abp. 13 Sept. (Lamb., Reg. Cranmer f. 235b). Trans. to Chester 1541.

M. Arthur Bulkeley D.Cn. & C.L. 1541–1553.

Lic. el. gr. 23 Oct. 1541 (*L. & P.* XVI No. 1391 (7)). El. 18 Nov. (Lamb., Reg. Cranmer f. 272). Royal assent 11 Dec. (*L. & P.* XVI No. 1488 (14)). Royal mand. to consecrate 11 Dec. (*ibid.*). Conf. by abp. 20 Dec. (Lamb., Reg. Cranmer f. 171b). Temps. 11 Feb. 1542 (*L. & P.* XVII No. 137 (29)). Oath of allegiance to k. and royal supremacy 18 Feb. (Lamb., Reg. Cranmer f. 277b). Cons. in St Paul's, London, 19 Feb. (*ibid.* f. 178). D. before 23 March 1553 (*ibid.* ff. 136b–137).

---

[1] So *Emden, Reg. Ox.* I 624. He is called a Dominican friar by Knowles (*Religious Orders in England* (Cambridge, 1948–59) III 493).

[2] Skevington had lic. to retain the abbey of Beaulieu *in commendam* (*Emden, Reg. Ox.* III 1707–8).

DEANS OF BANGOR

Adam 1328.
Occ. 28 Jan. and 26 Feb. 1328 (Cant., Reg. Q f. 172).[1]

Hywel ap Goronwy ?–1371.
Occ. 21 Apr. 1371 when prov. to bpc. of Bangor (Lamb., Reg. Wittlesey ff. 136b–137).

M. John Martyn 1382.
John occ. 31 July 1371 (Lamb., Reg. Wittlesey f. 136b). John Martyn occ. 28 Sept. 1382 (*CPR. 1381–1385* p. 442).

Walter de Swaffham 1389–?
Estate ratif. 25 May 1389 (*CPR. 1388–1392* p. 29). Royal gr. 20 July (*ibid.* p. 84).

William Clyve ?–1396.
Exch. deanery and preb. in Bangor with Philip Clyffeld for ch. of Woolaston, Glos., 17 Nov. 1396 (*Reg. Trefnant* p. 190).

Philip Clyffeld 1396–?
By exch. Nov. 1396.

David Daron 1397.
Estate ratif. 7 Nov. 1397 (*CPR. 1396–1399* p. 225).

William Pollard ?–1410.
Exch. deanery with Henry Henore for ch. of Newchurch, Kent, 10 June 1410 (Lamb., Reg. Arundell II f. 58).

Henry Henore 1410–1413.
By exch. June 1410. D. before 9 June 1413 (*Reg. Nicholls* p. 95).

Roger Wodele 1413–1416.
Coll. 9 June 1413 (*Reg. Nicholls* p. 95). Exch. deanery with John Vautort for ch. of St Mary, Colchester, Essex, 21 Sept. 1416 (*ibid.* pp. 104–5).

John Vautort 1416–?
By exch. Sept. 1416.

M. Nigel Bondeby B.Cn.L. 1423, 1436.
Occ. 15 March 1423 (*CPL.* VII 277). Occ. 26 Nov. 1436 (*Reg. Chichele* I 121).[2]

M. Hugh Alcock 1464.
Occ. 3 Oct. 1464 (*CPR. 1461–1467* p. 357).

M. Huw Morgan B.Cn.L. 1468.
Occ. 12 Dec. 1468 (*CPR. 1467–1477* p. 134).[3]

Richard Cyffin 1480.
Held deanery c. 1480 (*Williams* p. 319).

M. David[4] Yale B.C.L. 1502.
Occ. 1502 (*Report on MSS. in the Welsh Language* (Hist. MSS. Comm., 48, 1898–1910) II i 95).

---

[1] There is no evidence that Elias ap Kenric held the deanery 1353, as stated by Le Neve-Hardy.
[2] There is no evidence that John Martin held the deanery 1445, as stated by Le Neve-Hardy.
[3] There is no evidence that Nicholas Rewys held the deanery 1474 as stated by Le Neve-Hardy.
[4] He occ. here as Richard Yale, but this must be a confusion with Christian names, because David Yale succeeded Richard Cowland as portionary in the ch. of Llandinam, Montgom., 6 Oct. 1503, which suggests that they had exch. benefices. David Yale held a preb. in Bangor 1509 (*Report on MSS. in the Welsh Language* (Hist. MSS. Comm., 48, 1898–1910) II i 95).

M. **Richard Cowland** B.Cn.L. 1503–?
Adm. 18 Sept. 1503[1] (Lamb., Reg. Warham II f. 219b). Occ. 12 Sept. 1504 (*ibid.* f. 216). ? Held deanery until d., Sept. 1506 (*Emden, Reg. Ox.* I 505).

M. **John Glynn** ?–1535.
Occ. 28 Feb. 1509 (Lamb., Reg. Warham II f. 255). D. before 10 June 1535 (PCC 25 Hogen).

M. **Robert Evans** B.C.L. ?–1554.
Occ. 1535 (*Valor* IV 416). Depriv. before 28 Nov. 1554 (*Canterbury Institutions Sede Vacante* (Kent Records, viii) p. 5).[2]

CHANCELLORS OF BANGOR

M. **Huw Elis** B.Cn. & C.L. 1504, 1509.
Occ. 12 Sept. 1504 and 28 Feb. 1509 (Lamb., Reg. Warham II ff. 216, 255).

M. **William Glynn** D.Cn. & C.L. 1525, 1534.
Occ. 1525 (Nat. Libr. Wales, B/BR/1 f. 15). Occ. 26 June 1534 (*L. & P.* VII No. 889).

John Huws 1534.
Occ. 24 July 1534 (Lamb., Reg. Cranmer f. 238b).

PRECENTORS OF BANGOR

M. **John Gregger** 1504.
Occ. 12 Sept. 1504 (Lamb., Reg. Warham II f. 216).

M. **Thomas Ireland** 1509.
Occ. 28 Feb. 1509 (Lamb., Reg. Warham II f. 255).

John Robyns 1534.
Occ. 24 July 1534 (Lamb., Reg. Cranmer f. 238b).

TREASURERS OF BANGOR

M. **Richard Bangor** B.Cn.L. ?–1518.
Occ. 10 Sept. 1504 (Lamb., Reg. Warham II f. 215b). D. before 23 July 1518 (Nat. Libr. Wales, B/BR/1 f. 6b).

M. **Thomas David** M.A. 1518–?
Coll. 23 July 1518 (Nat. Libr. Wales, B/BR/1 f. 6b).

Lewis Newburgh ?–1554.
Occ. 1535 (*Valor* IV 417). Res. before 2 Aug. 1554 (Nat. Libr. Wales, B/BR/2 f. 14b).

---

[1] Possibly by exch. with David Yale. See p. 6 n. 4.
[2] Evans must have been restored to the deanery as he occ. as dn. at his d., 1570 (Nat. Libr. Wales, B/BR/2 f. 30).

ARCHDEACONS OF BANGOR

William 1328.
Occ. 26 Feb. 1328 (Cant., Reg. Q f. 172).[1]

Ithel ap Cynwrig 1345.
Occ. 12 March 1345 (*Cal. Anct. Correspondence* p. 228).

M. **Elias** 1345.
Occ. 21 Apr. 1345 (*Cal. Anct. Correspondence* p. 222).

Gervase ap Madog[2] 1367, 1391.
Occ. 16 Feb. 1367[3] (*Reg. Langham* p. 242). Estate ratif. 24 Sept. 1391 (*CPR. 1388–1392* p. 481).

Robert de Higham 1394, 1396.
Estate ratif. 1 Sept. 1394 (*CPR. 1391–1396* p. 494). Gr. royal pardon 26 July 1396 (*CPR. 1396–1399* p. 10).

Walter de Swaffham 1398–?
Iorwerth ap Madog ?–1399.[4]
Iorwerth Affeiriad ?–1399.[4]
Royal gr. to Swaffham 20 May 1398 (*CPR. 1396–1399* p. 347). Iorwerth ap Madog called 'late archdcn. of Bangor' 15 Jan. 1399 (*ibid.* p. 465). Iorwerth Affeiriad depriv. for plurality before 13 Apr. (*CPL.* v 239). Papal mand. s.d. to adm. Swaffham if found fit in Latin (*ibid.*). Estate ratif. 3 Jan. 1400 (*CPR. 1399–1401* p. 136).

Thomas ap Rhys 1411, 1417.
John de Carnyn 1411.
Thomas ap Rhys occ. 3 March 1411 (*CPL.* VI 187). Carnyn occ. 10 Sept. (*ibid.* p. 251). Thomas ap Rhys retained possession, occ. 10 Sept. 1417 (*Reg. Chichele* II 129).

Thomas Banastre ?–1433.
Occ. 22 Sept. 1431 (*CPL.* VIII 462). Exch. archdcnry with John Heygate for ch. of Great Brickhill, Bucks., 20 Feb. 1433 (Lincoln, Reg. XVII (Gray) ff. 48–48b).

M. **John Heygate** B.C.L. 1433–?
By exch. Feb. 1433.

Thomas Banastre (again) 1436.
Occ. 20 Apr. 1436 (*CPR. 1429–1436* p. 512).

John Parsons 1460, 1468.
Occ. 15 Oct. 1460 (*Reg. J. Stanbury*, ed. J. H. Parry and A. T. Bannister (Canterbury and York Soc., xxv) p. 57). Occ. 7 Jan. 1468 (*ibid.* p. 116).

---

[1] There is no evidence that David was archdcn. 1334 as stated by Le Neve-Hardy.

[2] See n. 4 below.

[3] There is no evidence that Gervase Fitz-David held the archdcnry 1351 and 1377 as stated by Le Neve-Hardy. He is possibly the same person as Gervase ap Madog since ap and Fitz have the same meaning. Many Welsh names give a genealogy to the bearers and he could have been Gervase ap Madog ap Dafydd and have shortened the name to Gervase (Iorwerth) ap Madog in Wales and to Gervase Fitz-David in England.

[4] Iorwerth ap Madog is probably the same person as Gervase ap Madog, archdcn. 1367, 1391, as Gervase is the normal English equivalent for Iorwerth. Iorwerth Affeiriad is possibly the same person also, as 'affeiriad' is the Welsh for priest or parson.

M. **Maurice Glynne** B.C.L. ?–1525.
Occ. 12 Sept. 1504 (Lamb., Reg. Warham II f. 216). D. 15/25 July 1525 (PCC 36 Bodfelde).

Thomas Runcorn[1] ?–1556.
Occ. 1529 (*L. & P.* IV iii No. 6047 p. 2701). D. 21 Sept./10 Oct. 1556 (PCC 22 Wrastley; Nat. Libr. Wales, B/BR/2 f. 13).

ARCHDEACONS OF ANGLESEY

M. **Einion Sais** ?–1309.
Res. this archdcnry 1309 when el. bp. of Bangor (*CPR. 1307–1313* p. 181).

Einion 1317.
Occ. 8 Dec. 1317 (*CPR. 1317–1321* p. 62).

Madog ap Meurig of Anglesey 1324.
Occ. 17 Sept. 1324 (*CPL.* II 241).

M. **Madog Hedwich** 1328.[2]
Occ. 28 Jan. and 28 Feb. 1328 (Cant., Reg. Q f. 172).

M. **John** 1345.
Occ. 21 Apr. 1345 (*Cal. Anct. Correspondence* p. 222).

Hywel ap Goronwy ?–1368.
Occ. 15 Apr. 1357 (Lamb., Reg. Islip f. 342b). D. before 25 Apr. 1368 (*CPL.* IV 69).

Thomas Harborough 1368–1395.
Prov. 25 Apr. 1368 (*CPL.* IV 69). D. before 13 June 1395 (*CPR. 1391–1396* p. 582).

John ap Rhys 1395–1398.
Walter de Swaffham ?–1398.
Royal gr. to John ap Rhys 13 June 1395 (*CPR. 1391–1396* p. 582). Estate of Swaffham ratif. 8 July and 5 Oct. (*ibid.* pp. 605, 622). John ap Rhys gr. lic. to sue for execution of prov. 29 Aug. 1397, had been prov. n.d. by pope Boniface IX (*CPR. 1396–1399* p. 193). Estate ratif. 13 Oct. (*ibid.* p. 224), but papal mand. 16 Apr. 1398 ordering him to resign (*CPL.* V 170). Swaffham probably res. 20 May when archdcn. of Bangor.

Evan ap Bleddyn 1405.
Occ. 19 Jan. 1405 (*Antiquitates Parochiales* p. 132).

Thomas Hywel ?–1410.
Res. this archdcnry before 23 Aug. 1410 (*Reg. Nicholls* p. 92).

John Wolde 1410–1413.
Coll. 23 Aug. 1410 (*Reg. Nicholls* p. 92). Res. before 17 Dec. 1413 (*ibid.* p. 96).

---

[1] An unnamed person, possibly Thomas Runcorn, was collated to the archdcnry 27 July 1525 (Nat. Libr. Wales, B/BR/1 f. 10b). Rowland Thomas was said by Le Neve-Hardy to have been archdcn. of Bangor 1534. No evidence has been found for this and confusion has probably arisen between his name and that of Thomas Runcorn, who appears to have held the archdcnry until his d., 1556.

[2] Matthew de Englefeld was said by Le Neve-Hardy to have been archdcn. of Anglesey in 1321 and 1327, but in 1328, when el. bp. of Bangor, he occ. only as canon (Cant., Reg. Q f. 172).

Thomas Hywel (again) 1413–?
Coll. 17 Dec. 1413 (*Reg. Nicholls* p. 96). Occ. 2 Aug. 1419 (*CPL.* VII 139).

M. **Andrew Holes** B.Cn. & C.L. 1428, 1440.
Occ. 30 Nov. 1428 (*CPL.* VIII 92). Occ. 24 Feb. 1440 (*ibid.* IX 81–2).

William Saundir 1446, 1452.
Occ. 7 July 1446 (*CPL.* IX 576). Occ. 12 Apr. 1452 (Lamb., Reg. Kempe ff. 216b–217).[1]

M. **William Moggys** M.A. 1469.
Occ. 29 June 1469 (*CPL.* XIII i 367). ? Held archdcnry until d., 8 March/13 Apr. 1497 (PCC 6 Horne).[2]

M. **Richard Bulkeley** B.C.L. ?–1524.
Occ. 12 Sept. 1504 (Lamb., Reg. Warham II f. 216). D. 5/6 Apr. 1524 (PCC 35 Bodfelde; Nat. Libr. Wales, B/BR/1 f. 10).

M. **William Glynn** D.Cn. & C.L. 1524–1537.
Coll. 6 Apr. 1524 (Nat. Libr. Wales, B/BR/1 f. 10). D. before 22 Oct. 1537 (*L. & P.* XII ii No. 1008 (29)).[3]

John Salisbury O.S.B. Bp. of Thetford. 1537–?
Coll. 20 Dec. 1537 (Nat. Libr. Wales, B/BR/1 f. 20). Occ. 24 Aug. 1539—called John Tetforde (Lamb., Reg. Cranmer f. 238b).

ARCHDEACONS OF MERIONETH

Tudur ab Adda
Tudur occ. 26 Feb. 1328 (Cant., Reg. Q f. 172). Tudur ab Adda d. as archdcn. after 24 June 1330 (*Brut y Tywysogyon* p. 126).

Tudur ap Dafydd 1358.
Tudur occ. 21 Apr. 1345 (*Cal. Anct. Correspondence* p. 222). Tudur ap Dafydd occ. 30 Jan. 1358 (Lamb., Reg. Islip f. 220).

Samuel de Wyk 1377, 1387.
John Sloleye 1387.
Wyk occ. 5 Jan. 1377 (P.R.O., E 179/3/1a).[4] Royal gr. to Sloleye 5 Feb. 1387 (*CPR. 1385–1389* p. 289). Estate of Wyk ratif. 17 Dec. (*ibid.* p. 378).

John ap Rhys ap Roppert ?–1404.
D. as archdcn. before 17 March 1404 (*CPL.* V 579).

M. **William Fychan** 1404–?
Mand. adm. 17 March 1404 if fit in Latin (*CPL.* V 579).

---

[1] There is no evidence that Huw Morgan held the archdcnry in 1468 as stated by Le Neve-Hardy. Morgan was dn. of Bangor in that year.
[2] There is no evidence that Nicholas ap Elys (ab Elis) held the archdcnry 1471 and 1474 as stated by Le Neve-Hardy.
[3] The collation of William Capon to the archdcnry 7 Aug. 1537 was cancelled, probably because Glynn was still living (Nat. Libr. Wales, B/BR/1 f. 20).
[4] In a diocesan return of aliens holding benefices. Wyk was the only alien holding a benefice in Bangor.

M. **Griffin le Yonge** D.Cn.L. 1405.
Occ. 19 Jan. 1405 (*Antiquitates Parochiales* p. 132).

Matthew Peyworden *or* **Wotton** ?–1410.
D. as archdcn. before 9 July 1410 (*Reg. Nicholls* p. 91).

Roger Hungarten 1410–?
Coll. 9 July 1410 (*Reg. Nicholls* p. 91).

M. **John Estcourt** B.C.L. 1416–?
Coll. 8 Apr. 1416 (*Reg. Nicholls* p. 104).

Richard Gele 1436.[1]
Estate ratif. 22 June 1436 (*CPR. 1429–1436* p. 496).

M. **Richard Bulkeley** B.C.L. 1485.
Occ. 3 Sept. 1485 (*CPL.* XIV 321).

M. **Richard Bromfield** B.Cn.L. 1504, 1513.
Occ. 12 Sept. 1504 (Lamb., Reg. Warham II f. 216). Occ. 26 Apr. 1513 (Nat. Libr. Wales, B/BR/1 f. 2).

M. **William Glynn** D.Cn. & C.L. ?–1524.
Res. this archdcnry 6 Apr. 1524 when archdcn. of Anglesey (Nat. Libr. Wales, B/BR/1 f. 10).

M. **William Roberts** B.C.L. 1524–1562.
Coll. 6 Apr. 1524 (Nat. Libr. Wales, B/BR/1 f. 10b). Treasurer 1554, but d. as archdcn. before 16 June 1562 (Nat. Libr. Wales, B/BR/2 f. 23).

PREBENDARIES OF BANGOR

There are two prebends of Bangor cathedral, Llanfair and Penmynydd, but during the period 1300–1541 no person was collated to a named prebend of Bangor. The prebendaries therefore have been arranged in chronological order from the dates of their collation or first occurrence.

William de Melton 1308.
Occ. 28 July 1308 (*CPL.* II 42).

Walter Reynolds ?–1308.
Vac. preb. 13 Oct. 1308 when bp. of Worcester (*Cal. Anct. Correspondence* pp. 178–9).

Thomas de Cauntebreg 1309.
Royal mand. 13 Jan. 1309 to adm. to preb. vac. by Walter Reynolds (*Cal. Anct. Correspondence* pp. 178–9; see above). Bp. replied that unable to collate Cauntebreg as had already adm. another person to preb. (*ibid.*).

M. **Adam de Murimuth** D.C.L. 1317.
Occ. 14 May 1317 (*CPL.* II 155).

Madog ap Meurig of Anglesey 1324.
Occ. 17 Sept. 1324 (*CPL.* II 241).

[1] There is no evidence that John Trygarn held the archdcnry 1422 and 1426 as stated by Le Neve-Hardy.

Matthew de Archllechwedd 1328.
Occ. 28 Jan. 1328 (Cant., Reg. Q f. 172).

Einion ap Tegwareth 1328.
Occ. 28 Jan. 1328 (Cant., Reg. Q f. 172).

John ap Gruffudd 1328.
Occ. 28 Jan. 1328 (Cant., Reg. Q f. 172).

M. Dafydd de Guellt 1328.
Occ. 27 Feb. and 18 May 1328 (Cant., Reg. Q ff. 171–171b, 160b).

M. Dafydd de Rhuddallt 1328.
Occ. 27 Feb. 1328 (Cant., Reg. Q ff. 171–171b).

M. Thomas Fastolf 1330–1340.
Adm. Dec. 1330 (Norwich, Reg. Ayremynne f. 39). Vac. preb. 21 Aug. 1340 when archdcn. of Norwich (*CPL.* II 547). Succeeded by Robert de Tresk (*ibid.* III 182; see below).

M. John Trefor B.Th. 1343–1346.
Prov. 20 Nov. 1343 (*CPL.* III 100). Bp. of St Asaph 1346.

Robert de Tresk 1344–1351.
Prov. 18 June 1344 to preb. vac. by Thomas Fastolf (*CPL.* III 182; see above). D. before 8 March 1351 (*CPL.* III 415). Succeeded by Hugh de Monyngton (see below).

Edmund Trefor 1347–?
Prov. 11 Apr. 1347 (*CPP.* I 107).

M. Hugh de Monyngton D.Th. 1351–?
Prov. 8 March 1351 to preb. vac. by Robert de Tresk (*CPL.* III 415; see above).

M. Ithel ap Robert B.C.L. ?–1402.
Occ. 17 Aug. 1357 (*CPP.* I 300–1). D. before 5 Feb. 1402 (*CPL.* V 485—called Ippart ap Robert). Succeeded by Thomas de Everdoun and John ap Goronwy Goch (see below p. 14).

M. William Loryng B.C.L. ?–1415.
Occ. 1 Sept. 1363 (*CPP.* I 452). Estate ratif. 16 Oct. 1386 (*CPR. 1385–1389* p. 221). Res. before 8 Oct. 1415 (*Reg. Nicholls* pp. 102–3). Succeeded by Nicholas Julian (see below p. 14).

M. Ralph de Ryngstede B.C.L. 1366.
Occ. 10 Oct. 1366 (*Reg. Langham* p. 76).

Thomas Delves 1366.
Occ. 25 Oct. 1366 (*Reg. Langham* p. 97).

Thomas de Lynton ?–1375.
Exch. preb. with John de Carleton for ch. of Allington, Lincs., 19 Feb. 1375 (Lincoln, Reg. X (Buckingham) ff. 308–308b; see below).

John de Carleton 1375–1380.
By exch. with Thomas de Lynton for ch. of Allington, Lincs., 19 Feb. 1375 (Lincoln, Reg. X (Buckingham) ff. 308–308b; see above). Exch. preb. with William de Humblestane for free chap. of Burley, Rut., 25 June 1380 (Lincoln, Reg. X (Buckingham) f. 326; see below p. 13).

William de Humblestane 1380–1408.

By exch. with John de Carleton for free chap. of Burley, Rut., 25 June 1380 (Lincoln, Reg. x (Buckingham) f. 326; see above p. 12). D. before 19 Oct. 1408 (*Reg. Nicholls* p. 87). Succeeded by William (see below p. 14).

William Seman ?–1395.

Occ. 25 July 1387 (*CPR. 1385–1389* p. 353). Exch. preb. with Nicholas Stoke for ch. of Normanby-le-Wold, Lincs., 23 Oct. 1395 (Lincoln, Reg. xi (Buckingham) ff. 79–79b; see below).

Griffin Tresgoet ?–1389.

Vac. preb. before 22 Nov. 1389 (*CPR. 1388–1392* p. 156). Succeeded by John de Burton (see below).

John de Burton 1389.

Estate ratif. 22 Nov. 1389 in preb. vac. by Griffin Tresgoet (*CPR. 1388–1392* p. 156; see above).

Nicholas Stoke 1395–?

By exch. with William Seman for ch. of Normanby-le-Wold, Lincs., 23 Oct. 1395 (Lincoln, Reg. xi (Buckingham) ff. 79–79b; see above). Mand. adm. 25 Nov. (Lincoln, Reg. xi (Buckingham) f. 79b).

William Clyve ?–1396.

Exch. deanery and preb. in Bangor with Philip Clyffeld for ch. of Woolaston, Glos., 17 Nov. 1396 (*Reg. Trefnant* p. 190; see below).

Philip Clyffeld 1396–?

By exch. with William Clyve for ch. of Woolaston, Glos., 17 Nov. 1396 (*Reg. Trefnant* p. 190; see above).

Ieuan ap Dafydd Fychan ?–1398.

Vac. preb. before 5 March 1398 (*CPR. 1396–1399* p. 258). Succeeded by Gruffudd Trefor (see below).

Gruffudd Trefor ?–1410.

Estate ratif. 5 March 1398 in preb. vac. by Ieuan ap Dafydd Fychan (*CPR. 1396–1399* p. 258; see above). D. before 5 Feb. 1410 (*Reg. Nicholls* p. 90). Succeeded by John Brampton (see below p. 14).

M. Lewis Aber ?–1398.

Vac. preb. 21 Aug. 1398 when el. bp. of Bangor (*CPL.* v 99; *CPR. 1396–1399* p. 460). Succeeded by Richard Prentys and Robert Egerley (see below).

Richard Prentys 1398.

Royal gr. 9 Oct. 1398 of preb. vac. by Lewis Aber (*CPR. 1396–1399* p. 460; see above). Vac. preb. before 25 Nov. (*CPR. 1396–1399* p. 451). Succeeded by Robert Egerley (see below).

Robert Egerley 1398–?

Royal gr. 25 Nov. 1398 of preb. vac. by Lewis Aber (*CPR. 1396–1399* p. 451; see above).

Thomas de Lenia[1] ?–1399.

Vac. preb. before 23 Jan. 1399 (*CPR. 1396–1399* p. 455). Succeeded by Thomas Martyn (see below p. 14).

---

[1] Thomas de Lenia and Thomas Llyn (see p. 14) are possibly the same person, but as there is insufficient evidence for this identification the names have been given separately.

Thomas Martyn 1399–?

Royal gr. 23 Jan. 1399 of preb. vac. by Thomas de Lenia (*CPR. 1396–1399* p. 455; see above p. 13).

Thomas Llyn¹ ?–1400.

Vac. preb. before 18 Nov. 1400 (*CPR. 1399–1401* p. 363). Succeeded by Griffin le Yonge (see below).

M. Griffin le Yonge B.Cn. & C.L. 1400, 1404.

Estate ratif. 18 Nov. 1400 in preb. vac. by Thomas Llyn (*CPR. 1399–1401* p. 363; see above). Yonge had been prov. to canonry with reservn. of preb. c. 17 Dec. 1399 (*CPL.* v 445–6). Occ. 27 March 1404 (*ibid.* p. 621). Officially bp. of Bangor 1407–1414 (see p. 4). Possibly retained preb. until 1414 when bp. of Ross, Scotland, or until 1423 when bp. of Hippo (*Eubel* I 446, 288)—had been prov. to bpc. of Ross by schismatic pope Benedict XIII. Succeeded in preb. by John Tylton *senior* n.d. (see below p. 15).

Thomas de Everdoun 1402.

Prov. 5 Feb. 1402 to preb. vac. by Ithel ap Robert (*CPL.* v 485; see above p. 12). Vac. preb. before 20 Feb. (*CPL.* v 616). Succeeded by John ap Goronwy Goch (see below).

John ap Goronwy Goch 1402–?

Mand. 20 Feb. 1402 to adm. to preb. vac. by Ithel ap Robert (*CPL.* v 616; see above p. 12).

John Wotton ?–1409.

Occ. 11 Nov. 1404 (*CPL.* VI 31). D. before 3 Aug. 1409 (PCC 19 Marche; *Reg. Nicholls* p. 107). Succeeded by Thomas Knight (see below).

M. William 1408–?

Coll. 19 Oct. 1408 to preb. vac. by William de Humblestane (*Reg. Nicholls* p. 87; see above p. 13).

John Brampton 1410–?

Coll. 5 Feb. 1410 to preb. vac. by Gruffudd Trefor (*Reg. Nicholls* p. 90; see above p. 13).

Thomas Knight 1410–1417.

Coll. 5 Feb. 1410 to preb. vac. by John Wotton (*Reg. Nicholls* p. 90; see above). D. before 6 Aug. 1417 (*Reg. Nicholls* p. 107). Succeeded by Edmund Nicholls (see below).

Thomas Hywel ?–1413.

Res. preb. Dec. 1413 when archdcn. of Anglesey (*Reg. Nicholls* p. 97). Succeeded by Thomas West (see below).

Thomas West 1414–?

Coll. 12 Jan. 1414 to preb. vac. by Thomas Hywel (*Reg. Nicholls* p. 97; see above).

Nicholas Julian 1415–?

Coll. 8 Oct. 1415 to preb. vac. by William Loryng (*Reg. Nicholls* pp. 102–3; see above p. 12).

Edmund Nicholls 1417–1422.

Coll. 6 Aug. 1417 to preb. vac. by Thomas Knight (*Reg. Nicholls* p. 107; see above). Exch. preb. and archdcnry of St Davids with William Ryley for ch. of

¹ See p. 13 n. 1.

Hemingford Abbots, Hunts., 12/22/24 Nov. 1422 (Lincoln, Reg. XVI (Fleming) ff. 112–113; see below).

Thomas Faukes 1422.
Occ. 7 Jan. 1422 (*CPL*. VII 223).

M. William Ryley B.Cn.L. 1422–1424.
By exch. with Edmund Nicholls for ch. of Hemingford Abbots, Hunts., 12/22/24 Nov. 1422 (Lincoln, Reg. XVI (Fleming) ff. 112–113; see above p. 14). D. before 19 May 1424 (*CPR. 1422–1429* p. 195). Succeeded by John Pye (see below).

M. John Dalton B.Cn. & C.L. 1423.
Occ. 1 June and 4 Sept. 1423 (*CPL*. VII 277, 304).

M. John Graystok B.Cn.L. 1423, 1450.
Occ. 1 June 1423 (*CPL*. VII 276). Occ. 24 Nov. 1450 (*ibid*. X 74).

John Pye 1424–?
Royal gr. 19 May 1424 of preb. vac. by William Ryley (*CPR. 1422–1429* p. 195; see above).

John Tylton *senior* ?–1424.
Vac. preb. formerly held by Griffin le Yonge before 4 July 1424 (*CPR. 1422–1429* p. 202; see above p. 14). Succeeded by John Tylton *junior* (see below).

John Tylton *junior* 1424–?
Royal gr. 4 July 1424 of preb. vac. by John Tylton *senior* (*CPR. 1422–1429* p. 202; see above).

William Saundir 1446.
Occ. 7 July 1446 (*CPL*. IX 576).

M. Ralph Heithcote B.Cn.L. 1482.
Occ. 23 July 1482 (*CPL*. XIII ii 807).

Richard Grygg 1509.
Occ. 12 Feb. 1509 (Lamb., Reg. Warham II f. 255).

M. Richard Myrion 1509.
Occ. 12 Feb. 1509 (Lamb., Reg. Warham II f. 255).

M. Robert Pyldeston ?–1527.
Occ. 12 Feb. 1509 (Lamb., Reg. Warham II f. 255). D. before 28 Aug. 1527 (Nat. Libr. Wales, B/BR/1 f. 5b). Succeeded by Dafydd ap Gruffudd (see below p. 16).

M. Dafydd Trefor 1509.
Occ. 28 Feb. 1509 (Lamb., Reg. Warham II f. 255).

M. David Yale B.C.L.? –1530.
Occ. 28 Feb. 1509 (Lamb., Reg. Warham II f. 255). Res. 1530 (Nat. Libr. Wales, B/BR/1 f. 19b). Succeeded by William Knight (see below p. 16).

M. Thomas Ireland ?–1520.
Res. preb. before 7 June 1520 (Nat. Libr. Wales, B/BR/1 f. 7b). Succeeded by Dafydd ap Gruffudd (see below).

Dafydd ap Gruffudd 1520–1527.
Coll. 7 June 1520 to preb. vac. by Thomas Ireland (Nat. Libr. Wales, B/BR/1 f. 7b; see above). Res. before 28 Aug. 1527 when obtained preb. vac. by Robert Pyldeston (Nat. Libr. Wales, B/BR/1 f. 5b; see below p. 16 and above).

Dafydd ap Gruffudd 1527–?
Coll. 28 Aug. 1527 to preb. vac. by Robert Pyldeston (Nat. Libr. Wales, B/BR/1 f. 5b; see above p. 15).

M. William Knight D.C.L. 1530–1541.
Coll. 1530 to preb. vac. by David Yale (Nat. Libr. Wales, B/BR/1 f. 19b; see above p. 15). Bp. of Bath and Wells 1541.

M. Arthur Bulkeley D.Cn.L. ?–1541.
Occ. 12 Feb. 1534 (Lamb., Reg. Cranmer f. 160).[1] Bp. of Bangor 1541.

M. William Cleyburgh D.Cn. & C.L. 1534.
Occ. 12 Feb. 1534 (Lamb., Reg. Cranmer f. 160).[1] D. before 30 May (Chichester, Reg. Sherborne II f. 74).

Huw ap Robert ?–1554.
Occ. 12 Feb. 1534 (Lamb., Reg. Cranmer f. 160).[1] Depriv. before 4 June 1554 (Nat. Libr. Wales, B/BR/2 f. 13b).

John Huws 1534.
Occ. 12 Feb. 1534 (Lamb., Reg. Cranmer f. 160).[1]

M. John Huws *or* **ap Hywel** B.Th. 1534.
Occ. 12 Feb. 1534 (Lamb., Reg. Cranmer f. 160).[1]

Dafydd Llwyd 1534, 1535.
Occ. 12 Feb. 1534 (Lamb., Reg. Cranmer f. 160). Occ. as preb. 1535 (*Valor* IV 418).

Lewis Newburgh 1534.
Occ. 12 Feb. 1534 (Lamb., Reg. Cranmer f. 160).[1]

John Robyns 1534, 1535.
Occ. 12 Feb. 1534 (Lamb., Reg. Cranmer f. 160). Occ. as preb. 1535 (*Valor* IV 418).

M. William Capon D.Th. 1535, 1539.
Occ. 1535 (*Valor* IV 417). Occ. 24 July 1539 (Lamb., Reg. Cranmer f. 238b).

Dafydd ap Madog 1535, 1541.
Occ. 1535 (*Valor* IV 417). Occ. 18 Nov. 1541 (Lamb., Reg. Cranmer f. 273).

Huw Goch 1539, 1541.
Occ. 24 July 1539 and 18 Nov. 1541 (Lamb., Reg. Cranmer ff. 238b, 273).

Lewis ap Tudur 1541.
Occ. 18 Nov. 1541 (Lamb., Reg. Cranmer f. 273).

CANONS WITH EXPECTATION OF PREBENDS

Dafydd de Rudalbach 1318–?
Prov. 20 July 1318 (*CPL.* II 176).

M. John Gruffudd Ddu Sch.Cn.L. 1358–?
Prov. 20 Sept. 1358 (*CPP.* I 332). Occ. 21 Jan. 1361 (*ibid.* p. 362).

[1] A list is given in abp. Cranmer's reg., 12 Feb. 1534, of prebendaries and canons of Bangor (Lamb., Reg. Cranmer f. 160). As no distinction has been made between the two offices, all persons who occur at that date have been listed here among the prebendaries, not among the canons of Bangor.

Robert de Shardlowe 1361–?
Prov. 20 Jan. 1361 (*CPP.* I 365).

M. Thomas Howe of Erpingham B.C.L. 1363–?
Prov. 26 June 1363 (*CPP.* I 437). ? Until d., 23 March/14 Apr. 1383 (*Emden, Reg. Camb.* p. 317).

Hywel ap Madog 1390–?
Prov. 22 June 1390 (*CPL.* IV 337). Occ. 17 Feb. 1391 (*ibid.* p. 144).

CANONS OF BANGOR

Hugh de Leminster 1304.
Occ. 23 Feb. 1304 (*Reg. Corbridge* I 272).

M. Gregory ab Einion 1309.
Occ. 18 June 1309 (P.R.O., C 84/16/24).

M. Matthew de Neuyn 1309.
Occ. 18 June 1309 (P.R.O., C 84/16/24).

Einion ap Meurig 1328.
Occ. 28 Jan. 1328 (Cant., Reg. Q f. 172).

M. Matthew de Englefeld ?–1328.
Occ. 28 Jan. 1328 (Cant., Reg. Q f. 172). El. bp. of Bangor 26 Feb.

Madog Ddu 1330.
Occ. 6 July 1330 (*CPL.* II 319).

David Philippi 1330.
Occ. 6 July 1330 (*CPL.* II 319).

John de Dyffrynclwyt 1343.
Occ. 22 July 1343 (*CPL.* III 85).

M. Robert Pollard ?–1355.
D. as can. before Nov. 1355 (*Black Prince's Reg.* III 494).

Madog ap Dafydd Llwyd 1358.
Occ. 13 Sept. 1358 (*CPL.* III 601).

M. William Fychan 1405.
Occ. 19 Jan. 1405 (*Antiquitates Parochiales* p. 132).

M. Hugh Alcock 1430, 1465.[1]
Occ. 27 June 1430 and 8 May 1465 (Brit. Mus., Add. Charters 43501, 43537).

M. Robert Appulby B.Cn. & C.L. 1440.
Occ. 5 March 1440 (*CPL.* IX 78).

Huw Tregar 1441.
Occ. 29 Apr. 1441 (*CPL.* IX 191).

M. William Conwey 1464.
Occ. 3 Oct. 1464 (*Foedera* V ii 127).

M. Richard Fychan 1504, 1509.
Occ. 12 Sept. 1504 and 28 Feb. 1509 (Lamb., Reg. Warham II ff. 216, 255).

[1] Alcock occ. as dn. of Bangor 3 Oct. 1464 but evidently retained his canonry.

Llandaff 1300-1541

MANUSCRIPT MATERIAL

National Library of Wales, Aberystwyth
MS. 17110 E. Liber Landavensis.

Canterbury Cathedral Library
Registers A, S.

Lambeth Palace Library
The registers of the archbishops of Canterbury from Reynolds to Cranmer, 1314–1555.

Somerset House
PCC: Registers of wills proved in the prerogative court of Canterbury.

M. John de Monmouth D.Th. 1294–1323.

Prov. 2 Oct. 1294 (*Reg. Winchelsey* I 7). Appointed by abp.[1] 14 Oct. (*ibid.* pp. 5–8). Temps. 4 Apr. 1295 (*CPR. 1292–1301* p. 132). Abp. requested pope Boniface VIII 10 Oct. for instructions before proceeding with cons. of Monmouth since bp. had been prov. by pope Celestine V, who abdicated 13 Dec. 1294 and whose acts were revoked by pope Boniface VIII (*Reg. Winchelsey* II 513–14). Monmouth cons. 10 Feb. 1297 by abp. at Canterbury (Cant., Reg. A f. 311b/255b). D. 8 Apr. 1323 (Nat. Libr. Wales, MS. 17110 E f. 121b).

[M. Alexander de Monmouth 1323.]

John de Eglescliffe O.P. 1323–1347.

Lic. el. gr. 31 May 1323 (*CPR. 1321–1324* p. 293). El. of Monmouth 25 June (P.R.O., C 84/20/20). Royal assent sought 7 July (*ibid.*), gr. 15 July (*CPR. 1321–1324* p. 326). El. set aside by prov. of Eglescliffe, trans. from Connor, Ireland, 20 June (Lamb., Reg. Reynolds f. 234b). Temps. 13 Aug. 1324 (*CPR. 1324–1327* p. 11). D. 2 Jan. 1347 (Nat. Libr. Wales, MS. 17110 E f. 121b).

[John de Coventry 1347.]

M. John Pascal O.Carm., D.Th. 1347–1361.

Coventry el. by chapt. n.d. (Nat. Libr. Wales, MS. 17110 E f. 121b). Pascal prov. 19 Feb. 1347 (*CPL.* III 236). Royal assent to el. of Coventry 16 March (*Black Prince's Reg.* I 59). Pascal retained bpc., cons. n.d. by bp. of Porto (*R.S.A.*). Profession to abp. 4 June (Cant., Reg. A f. 311b/255b). Temps. 2/7 July (*Black Prince's Reg.* I 105; *CPR. 1345–1348* p. 350). D. 11 Oct. 1361 (Lamb., Reg. Islip f. 239).

Roger Cradock O.F.M. 1361–1382.

Trans. from Waterford and Lismore, Ireland, 15 Dec. 1361 (Lamb., Reg. Islip f. 239b). Profession to abp. 31 March 1362 at Mayfield, Suss. (*ibid.*). Mand. to deliver spir. s.d. (*ibid.* f. 240). D. before 16 Aug. 1382 (*CPR. 1381–1385* p. 173).

M. Thomas Rushooke O.P., M.Th. 1383–1385.

Lic. el. gr. 16 Aug. 1382 (*CPR. 1381–1385* p. 173). Prov. 14/15 Jan. 1383 (P.R.O., Papal Bulls 62 (12); Lamb., Reg. Courtenay f. 318). Lic. *alibi cons.* 16 Jan. (Lamb., Reg. Courtenay f. 318b). Temps. 2 Apr. (*CPR. 1381–1385* p. 266). Profession to abp. 10 Apr. (Lamb., Reg. Courtenay f. 318). Spir. s.d. (*ibid.* f. 318b). Cons. 3 May at London (*ibid.*). Trans. to Chichester 1385.

M. William de Bottlesham O.P., D.Th. Bishop of Bethlehem. 1385–1389.

Prov. 16 Oct./2 Dec. 1385 (P.R.O., Papal Bulls 62 (11); *Eubel* I 304). Temps. 21 Aug. 1386 (*CPR. 1385–1389* p. 209). Trans. to Rochester 1389.

---

[1] 'Iste [Monmouth] non fuit electus set dictus dominus R. archiepiscopus dei gratia sedis apostolice contulit sibi dictum episcopatum Landavensem' (Cant., Reg. A f. 311b/255b).

M. Edmund Bromfield O.S.B., D.Th. 1389–1393.

Prov. after 27 Aug. 1389[1] (*Eubel* I 304). Temps. 17 Dec. (*CPR. 1388–1392* p. 170). Cons. at Rome 20 Jan. 1390 (*R.S.A.*). D. 11 June 1393 (P.R.O., C 84/35/40).

Robert Tideman of Winchcombe O.Cist. 1393–1395.

Lic. el. sought 15 June 1393 (P.R.O., C 84/35/40). Lic. el. gr. 5 July (*CPR. 1391–1396* p. 300). Letter from k. to chapt. at Llandaff July/Aug. recommending el. of Tideman (*Anglo-Norman Letters and Petitions*, ed. M. D. Legge (Oxford, 1941) p. 61). El. of Tideman notified to k. 12 Aug. (P.R.O., C 84/35/43). Royal assent 18 Aug. (*CPR. 1391–1396* p. 319). Prov. 13 Oct. (*CPL.* IV 459). Assent of parliament Feb. 1394 (*Rot. Parl.* III 317). Temps. 3 July and 24 Oct. (*CPR. 1391–1396* pp. 325, 446). Trans. to Worcester 1395.

M. Andrew Barret D.C.L. 1395–1396.

Prov. 2/4 June 1395 (P.R.O., Papal Bulls 41 (2); *Eubel* I 304). Temps. 25 Aug. (*CPR. 1391–1396* p. 614). Cons. n.d. at Rome (*R.S.A.*). D. before 12 Apr. 1396 (*CPL.* IV 539).

John de Burghill O.P. 1396–1398.

Prov. 12 Apr. 1396 (*CPL.* IV 539). Custody of temps. gr. 31 May (*CPR. 1391–1396* p. 713). Plenary restitution of temps. 15 June (*ibid.* p. 683). Cons. n.d. at Rome (*R.S.A.*). Trans. to Coventry and Lichfield 1398.

M. Thomas Peverel O.Carm., B.Th. 1398–1407.

Trans. from Leighlin, Ireland, 12 July 1398 (*CPL.* V 88). Temps. 16 Nov. (*CPR. 1396–1399* pp. 446–7).[2] Trans. to Worcester 1407.

M. John la Zouche O.F.M., D.Th. 1407–1423.

Called bp. el. of Llandaff 13 Nov. 1407 (*CPL.* VI 113). Temps. 7 June 1408 (*CPR. 1405–1408* p. 442). Cons. 12 Aug. (*R.S.A.*). D. before 28 Apr. 1423 (*CPR. 1422–1429* p. 82).

[**M. John Fulford** D.Th. 1423–1425.]
M. John Welles O.F.M., D.Th. 1425–1440.

Lic. el. gr. 28 Apr. 1423 (*CPR. 1422–1429* p. 82). Chapt. el. Fulford n.d., royal assent sought 6 May (P.R.O., C 84/42/47). Royal assent signified to pope 12 May (*CPR. 1422–1429* p. 97). El. set aside by prov. of Welles 9 July 1425 (*Reg. Chichele* I 88). Profession to abp. 15 Jan. 1426 (*ibid.*). Spir. and temps. s.d. (*ibid.* pp. 88–9; *CPR. 1422–1429* p. 318). D. before 17 Nov. 1440 (*CPR. 1436–1441* p. 488).

[**M. Reginald Boulers** O.S.B., D.Th. 1440.]
Nicholas Ashby O.S.B. 1440–1458.

Lic. el. gr. 17 Nov. 1440 (*CPR. 1436–1441* p. 488). Boulers nominated as bp. by k. 21 Nov. (*Official Correspondence of Thomas Bekynton* (R.S. 56) I 27–9). Boulers refused bpc. (*ibid.* p. 22). Ashby recommended to chapt. by k. 25 Dec. (*ibid.* pp. 31–2). Ashby prov. 17 Feb. 1441 (P.R.O., C 84/46/2). Royal assent signified to pope 18 March (*CPR. 1436–1441* p. 511). Temps. 15 Apr. (*ibid.* p. 541). Cons. 21 May (*R.S.A.*). Profession to abp. 24 May (*Reg. Chichele* I 126). D. before 19 June 1458 (*CPL.* XI 358).

---

[1] Bottlesham was trans. to Rochester 27 Aug. 1389 (Lamb., Reg. Courtenay f. 328). Bromfield must have been prov. to Llandaff after that date.

[2] It has been suggested that M. Adam de Usk was intended to oust Peverel from the bpc. c. 1406 as part of the policy of the followers of Owain Glyn Dŵr to create an all-Welsh episcopate (*Williams* p. 224).

M. **John Hunden** O.P., D.Th. 1458–1476.

Prov. 19 June 1458 (*CPL.* XI 358). Lic. *alibi cons.* s.d. (*ibid.* p. 359). Temps. 25 Aug. (*CPR. 1452–1461* p. 431). Cons. n.d. at Rome (*R.S.A.*). Res. before 18 March 1476[1] (*CPL.* XIII ii 480, 482).

M. **John Smith** D.Th. 1476–1478.

Prov. c. 30 March 1476 (*CPL.* XIII ii 480). Lic. *alibi cons.* 17 July (Cant., Reg. S f. 277). Temps. 11 Sept. (*CPR. 1467–1477* p. 598). Cons. n.d. in England (*R.S.A.*). D. 29 Jan. 1478 (Brit. Mus., Cotton MS. Vitellius F. xii f. 276b).

M. **John Marshall** D.Th. 1478–1496.

Prov. 18 May 1478 (P.R.O., Papal Bulls 37 (2)). Lic. *alibi cons.* 6 Sept. (Cant., Reg. S f. 277). Temps. 18 Sept. (*CPR. 1476–1485* p. 122) and 18 Dec. (*Foedera* v iii 95). Cons. n.d. (*R.S.A.*). D. 3 Jan./23 Feb. 1496 (PCC 30 Vox).

M. **John Ingleby** O.Carth. 1496–1499.

Prov. 27 June 1496 (P.R.O., Papal Bulls 37 (36)). Temps. 2 Sept. (*CPR. 1494–1509* p. 76). Lic. *alibi cons.* 6 Sept. (Cant., Reg. S f. 408b). Cons. n.d. in England (*R.S.A.*). D. before 14 Nov. 1499 (*CPR. 1494–1509* p. 185).

Miles Sawley O.S.B. 1499–1516/17.

Custody of temps. gr. 14 Nov. 1499 (*CPR. 1494–1509* p. 185). Lic. *alibi cons.* 10 March 1500 (Cant., Reg. S f. 433b). Temps. 12 May (*CPR. 1494–1509* p. 206). Cons. n.d. by abp. (*R.S.A.*). D. 29 Nov. 1516/7 Jan. 1517 (PCC 26 Holder; Lamb., Reg. Warham II ff. 281b–282).

M. **George Athequa** O.P., D.Th. 1517–1537.

Prov. 7/11 Feb. 1517 (*L. & P.* II ii No. 2879; Lamb., Reg. Warham I f. 19b). Lic. *alibi cons.* 27 Feb. (Lamb., Reg. Warham I f. 19b). Cons. 8 March in St Paul's, London, by bp. of Hereford (*ibid.* f. 20). Spir. 9 March (*ibid.* ff. 20–20b). Temps. 22/23 Apr. (*L. & P.* II ii No. 3166). Res. before 2 March 1537 (*ibid.* XII i No. 795 (5)).

M. **Robert Holgate** O.Gilb.,[2] D.Th. Prior of Watton. 1537–1545.

Lic. el. gr. 2 March 1537 (*L. & P.* XII i No. 795 (5)). El. 8 March (*ibid.* No. 795 (30)). Royal assent 19 March (*ibid.*). Conf. by abp. 22 March (Lamb., Reg. Cranmer f. 199). Cons. by abp. 25 March (*ibid.* f. 200). Temps. 29 March (*L. & P.* XII i No. 795 (47)). Enthroned 12 June (Nat. Libr. Wales, MS. 17110 E f. 120). Abp. of York 1545.

ARCHDEACONS OF LLANDAFF

M. **Henry de Cranborne** *or* **Wager** 1289–?
Robert 1290.

Cranborne prov. 13 Dec. 1289 (*CPL.* I 508). Robert occ. 15 Sept. 1290 (*ibid.* p. 519). Cranborne retained possession, occ. 24 Apr. 1306 (*CPR. 1301–1307* p. 432).

M. **Alexander de Monmouth** 1323, 1337.

Occ. 15 July 1323 (*CPR. 1321–1324* p. 326). Occ. 8 March 1337 (*CPR. 1334–1338* p. 394).

---

[1] Hunden occ. as archdcn. of St Davids 18 March 1476 (*CPL.* XIII ii 482). After he res. the bpc. of Llandaff he was called 'a bishop in the universal church', 30 March 1476 (*ibid.* p. 80). He does not occur as a card. bp. (*Eubel* II), but had possibly been made a bp. *in partibus infidelium*.

[2] Holgate was Master of the Order of Gilbertines at the time of his el. to the bpc. of Llandaff. He had lic. to retain the priory of Watton, Yorks., *in commendam* with the bpc. (*L. & P.* XII i No. 795 (30)).

M. Richard de Halton 1338.
> Occ. 9 Oct. 1338 (*Memorials of Llandaff* p. 331).

John de Coventry ?–1361.
Thomas de Burgherssh 1347.
> Coventry occ. 16 March 1347 when el. bp. of Llandaff (*Black Prince's Reg.* I 59). Royal gr. to Burgherssh 20 May (*ibid.* p. 83). Coventry did not obtain bpc., regained archdcnry since occ. 16 Dec. 1348 (*CPL.* III 271). D. before 12 Nov. 1361 (Brit. Mus., Harley Charter 75. B. 42).

M. Henry Despenser B.C.L. 1361, 1364.
Robert de Walsham 1361–1368.
M. Thomas Banastre of Eltisley B.Cn. & C.L. 1363–?
M. Thomas de Southam Lic. C.L., B.Cn.L. 1366.
> Despenser and Walsham obtained archdcnry by royal gr. from the Prince of Wales during vac. of bpc., 11 Oct.–15 Dec. 1361 (*CPP.* I 490–1, 524). Banastre said to have been intruded into archdcnry by bp. Cradock, who was prov. 15 Dec. (*ibid.*). Prov. to archdcnry 1 June 1363 (*ibid.* p. 424). Despenser petitioned pope 20 Apr. 1364 that he should be permitted to retain archdcnry because Banastre had then res. at curia (*ibid.* pp. 490–1). Southam had been prov., n.d., petitioned pope 7 Apr. 1366 to be permitted to resign archdcnry, petition gr. since Walsham occ. 15 Apr. (*ibid.* p. 524). Exch. archdcnry with Richard Boule for ch. of Tettenhall Wood, Staffs., 11 Nov. 1368 (Lichfield, Reg. IV (Stretton) f. 60).

M. Richard Boule B.C.L. 1368–?
> By exch. Nov. 1368.

Thomas de Alston ?–1373.
> Exch. archdcnry and preb. of Caerau with John de Sulthorn for ch. of Aldington, Kent, 20 Dec. 1373 (Lamb., Reg. Wittlesey ff. 95–95b).

John de Sulthorn 1373–?
> By exch. Dec. 1373.

M. Robert de la More D.C.L. 1385, 1393.
> Occ. 5 June 1385 (Brit. Mus., Harley Charter 75. A. 33). Estate ratif. 5 Dec. 1391 (*CPR. 1388–1392* p. 505). Occ. Autumn 1393 (*Cardiff Records*, ed. J. H. Matthews (Cardiff, 1898–1911) I 160).

Thomas Orewelle 1396–?
> Royal gr. 25 March 1396 (*CPR. 1391–1396* p. 693). Estate ratif. 30 Oct. 1399 (*CPR. 1399–1401* p. 25). Thomas occ. 19 May 1409 (*CPR. 1408–1413* p. 78).

M. Robert Cole ?–1447.
> Exch. archdcnry with John Stradling for ch. of Edington, Wilts., 24 Sept. 1447 (Salis., Reg. Aiscough pt. i f. 109b).

M. John Stradling 1447–1454.
> By exch. Sept. 1447. Exch. archdcnry with Lewis Byford for ch. of North Tawton, Devon, 15 Nov. 1454 (Exeter, Reg. Lacy I ff. 285b–286).

M. Lewis Byford 1454–?
> By exch. Nov. 1454. Occ. 1 March 1477 (*Reg. Bourgchier* p. 214).[1]

---

[1] There is no evidence that Gundisalve Ferdinand held the archdcnry in 1499 and 1500 as stated by Le Neve-Hardy.

M. **John Quarre** 1529, 1541.

Occ. 1529 (*L. & P.* IV iii No. 6047 p. 2701). Occ. 25 June 1541 (*Registers of Thomas Wolsey, etc.*, ed. Sir H. C. Maxwell-Lyte (Somerset Record Soc., lv) pp. 90–1).

CHANCELLORS OF LLANDAFF

John de Coventry
Occ. as chancellor and treasurer n.d.,[1] but probably before 1347 when occ. as archdcn. of Llandaff (*Cartae et Munimenta de Glamorgan* IV 1266; see above p. 24, below p. 26).

William Barneby 1347.
Occ. 7 July 1347 (*CPL.* III 241).

M. **John de Middleton** 1361.
Occ. 18 Oct. 1361 (Lamb., Reg. Islip f. 239).

Thomas de Braundeston ?–1372.
Occ. 12 June 1367 (*Reg. Sudbury* II 510). Precentor 1372.

Henry Fouleshurst ?–1394.
Exch. chancellorship with Richard Wormebrugge for ch. of Newland, nr. Monmouth, Glos., 18/25 March/5 Apr. 1394 (*CPR. 1391–1396* pp. 390, 404; *Reg. Trefnant* p. 189).

Richard Wormebrugge 1394–1395.
By exch. March/Apr. 1394. Exch. chancellorship with Geoffrey Walker for ch. of Beechamwell, Norf., 22 July 1395 (Norwich, Reg. Despenser ff. 200b–201).

Geoffrey Walker *or* **Ludlowe** 1395–?
By exch. July 1395. Occ. 2 March 1397 (*CPL.* V 25).

Philip ap Llywellyn[2] 1423.
Occ. 24 Nov. 1423 (*CPL.* VII 281).

M. **Philip Lowys**[2] 1424, 1425.
Occ. 20 July 1424 and 10 July 1425 (*CPR. 1422–1429* pp. 213, 289–90).

Robert Thomas 1441.
Occ. 17 Feb. and 24 Aug. 1441 (*Reg. Chichele* I 125, 126).

William Brokeburn 1487.
Occ. 7 Nov. 1487 (*CPL.* XIV 258).

PRECENTORS OF LLANDAFF

John de Hale 1347–?
Royal gr. 30 July 1347 (*Black Prince's Reg.* I 91).

M. **Philip Ewyas** Sch.Cn. & C.L. 1359–1372.
Prov. to precentorship conf. 25 June 1359 (*CPP.* I 312, 344). D. before 10 Aug. 1372 (*CPL.* IV 178).

[1] The date of the document which is attested by John de Coventry as chancellor and treasurer of Llandaff has been eaten by rats.
[2] Philip ap Llywellyn and Philip Lowys are possibly the same person.

Thomas de Braundeston 1372–?
Mand. adm. 10 Aug. 1372 if found fit in Latin (*CPL.* IV 178).

Thomas Orewelle ?–1396.
Res. precentorship 25 March 1396 when archdcn. of Llandaff (*CPR. 1391–1396* p. 693).

M. Robert Boleyn 1396–1401.
Royal gr. 25 March 1396 (*CPR. 1391–1396* p. 693). Estate ratif. 30 Oct. 1399 (*CPR. 1399–1401* p. 25). Exch. precentorship with Adam Bacon for ch. of Achurch, Northants., 1 March 1401 (Lincoln, Reg. XIII (Beaufort) f. 221b/103b).

Adam Bacon 1401–?
By exch. March 1401.

M. Thomas Lavenham *or* **Moriel** Lic.Cn.L. ?–1427.[1]
Res. precentorship before 22 Sept. 1427 (*CPL.* VII 499).

M. — Hickman 1535.
Occ. 1535 (*Valor* IV 348).

TREASURERS OF LLANDAFF

Robert of St Fagans 1301.
Occ. 15 May 1301 (*Reg. Winchelsey* I 411).

M. Richard de Halton 1320, 1332.
Occ. 11 Nov. 1320 (*Reg. A. de Orleton*, ed. A. T. Bannister (Canterbury and York Soc., V) pp. 156–7). Occ. 26 Dec. 1332 (Nat. Libr. Wales, MS. 17110 E f. 116b). (Occ. as archdcn. 1338.)

John de Coventry[2]
Occ. as chancellor and treasurer n.d., but before 1347 when occ. as archdcn. (*Cartae et Munimenta de Glamorgan* IV 1266).

M. Richard de Haverisham D.C.L. 1348, 1349.
Occ. 12 July 1348 (*CPP.* I 133). Occ. 14 March 1349 (*CPR. 1348–1350* p. 315).

Thomas West ?–1360.
Exch. treasurership with John de Newenham for ch. of Ecton, Northants., 8 May 1360 (Lincoln, Reg. IX (Gynewell) f. 230b).

John de Newenham 1360–?
By exch. May 1360. Adm. 16 June (Lincoln, Reg. IX (Gynewell) f. 230b).

Peter de Gildesburgh ?–1366.
Exch. treasurership with Stephen de Navesby for ch. of Naseby, Northants., 12 May 1366 (Lincoln, Reg. X (Buckingham) f. 164b).

---

[1] Lavenham had res. the precentorship by 22 Sept. 1427, and appears to have obtained it about seven years earlier because it is stated that he 'had lately received papal dispensation to hold with the ch. of Biddenham, Beds., one other benefice, for seven years. After which he obtained the precentorship of Llandaff . . . and on resigning it the parish ch. of St Mary Binbrook, Lincs.' (*CPL.* VII 499).
[2] See p. 25 n. 1.

Stephen de Navesby 1366–1368.

By exch. May 1366. Exch. treasurership with Lewis of St Melans for ch. of Upper Hardres, Kent, 10 June 1368 (*Reg. Langham* pp. 304–6).

Lewis of St Melans 1368–?

By exch. June 1368. Mand. adm. 21 June (*Reg. Langham* p. 304).

John Rider ?–1402.

Exch. treasurership with John Hereford for ch. of Uppingham, Rut., 29 Nov. 1402 (Lincoln, Reg. XIII (Beaufort) ff. 234/110–234b/110b).

John Hereford *or* Carpenter 1402–?

By exch. Nov. 1402. Estate ratif. 5 May 1403 (*CPR. 1401–1405* p. 191).[1]

John ab Ieuan ?–1541/2.

Occ. 5 Sept. 1534 (*L. & P.* VII No. 1216 (7)). D. 1 Nov. 1541/6 Feb. 1542 (PCC 1 Spert).

PREBENDARIES OF CAERAU

Robert de Stretton 1347–?
Royal gr. 28 March 1347 (*Black Prince's Reg.* I 69).

Roger ?–1352.
D. as preb. before 23 July 1352 (*CPP.* I 229).

M. William de Bergevenny D.Th. 1352–?
Prov. 23 July 1352 (*CPP.* I 229). Had been prov. to canonry with reservn. of preb. 2 July 1343 (*CPL.* III 126). Engaged in litigation about a preb. in Llandaff 28 Jan. 1349 (*ibid.* p. 273). Possibly then claiming Caerau in opposition to Stretton, clerk of the Prince of Wales (see above).

Thomas de Alston ?–1373.
Exch. this preb. and archdcnry of Llandaff with John de Sulthorn for ch. of Aldington, Kent, 20 Dec. 1373 (Lamb., Reg. Wittlesey ff. 95–95b).

John de Sulthorn 1373–?
By exch. Dec. 1373.

Thomas Knight 1408.
Estate ratif. 18 July 1408 (*CPR. 1405–1408* p. 458).

John Rider 1411–?
Royal gr. 16 June 1411 (*CPR. 1408–1413* p. 297). Occ. 28 Apr. 1421 (*CPL.* VII 169).

John Houden ?–1434.
Exch. this preb. with John Vautort for preb. in chap. of St Mary and the Holy Angels, York minster, 24 June 1434 (York, Reg. Kempe f. 14).

John Vautort 1434–?
By exch. June 1434.

M. Richard Gwent D.Cn.L. 1535.
Occ. 1535 (*Valor* IV 348). ? Held preb. until d., 21 July 1543/11 Feb. 1544 (PCC 3 Pynnyng).

---

[1] There is no evidence that David Morgan held the treasurership 1480 as stated by Le Neve-Hardy.

PREBENDARIES OF FAIRWATER or THOMAS JONES

M. Thomas Ruggele[1]? –1429.
Res. this preb. before 23 Sept. 1429 (*Cat. Anct. Deeds* I 535).

M. Dafydd Lewes 1429–?
Obtained preb. after 23 Sept. 1429 (*Cat. Anct. Deeds* I 535).

PREBENDARIES OF FAIRWELL

No prebendaries of Fairwell have been found for the period 1300–1541.

PREBENDARIES OF LLANGWM

Robert Perle 1366.
Occ. 15 Oct. 1366 (*Reg. Langham* p. 24).

PREBENDARIES OF ST ANDREW or THOMAS BASSCHURCH

Nicholas de Hadham 1366.
Occ. 15 Nov. 1366 (*Reg. Langham* pp. 69–70).

John Grym ?–1372.
Exch. this preb. with Lawrence Morgan for ch. of Checkendon, Oxon., 30 Apr. 1372 (Lincoln, Reg. x (Buckingham) f. 356).

Lawrence Morgan 1372–?
By exch. Apr. 1372. Mand. adm. 10 May (Lincoln, Reg. x (Buckingham) f. 356).

John Attewater[2] ?–1411.
Exch. this preb. with John Payn for chap. of Wanborough, Wilts., 21 Feb. 1411 (Salis., Reg. Hallum ff. 22–22b).

John Payn[2] 1411–?
By exch. Feb. 1411.

PREBENDARIES OF ST CROSS or HENRY MORGAN

Henry de Fynyngleye 1366.
Occ. 15 Nov. 1366 (*Reg. Langham* p. 69).

John de Wythornwyk ?–1394.
Res. this preb. before 28 May 1394 (*CPR. 1391–1396* p. 415).

---

[1] It is possible that John Attewater and John Payn held this preb. 1411 (see n. 2).

[2] Attewater and Payn could have been prebendaries of Fairwater since the prebend which they exch. is called St Andrew or Fairwater (Salis., Reg. Hallum ff. 22–22b).

John Roland 1394–?
Royal gr. 28 May 1394 (*CPR. 1391–1396* p. 415). Estate ratif. 14 Oct. 1399 (*CPR. 1399–1401* p. 5).

M. Henry Morgan D.C.L. 1535.
Occ. 1535 (*Valor* IV 348).

PREBENDARIES OF ST DUBRITIUS

M. Nicholas de Newton B.Cn.L. 1366.
Occ. Sept. 1366 (*Reg. Langham* p. 46).

PREBENDARIES OF ST NICHOLAS *or* MASTER MAYO *or* HENRY III

Richard Passemer 1331.
Occ. as rector of St Nicholas, Llandaff,[1] 1 July 1331 (*CPL.* II 343).

M. William de Thinghull B.Cn. & C.L. ?–1353.
Exch. this preb. with Henry Motelet for ch. of Trowse, Norf., 18 Oct. 1353 (Norwich, Reg. Bateman f. 151b).

M. Henry Motelet 1353–?
By exch. Oct. 1353. Mand. adm. 4 Nov. (Norwich, Reg. Bateman ff. 151b–152). Occ., called can., 12 Dec. 1361 (Lamb., Reg. Islip f. 239b).

Thomas de Tunstable 1366.
Occ. 15 Nov. 1366 (*Reg. Langham* p. 71).

William de Pilton 1405.
Occ. 2 Feb. 1405 (*CPL.* VI 49).

John Prentys 1408–?
Royal gr. 5 March 1408 (*CPR. 1405–1408* p. 461). ? Held preb. until d., 28 May/28 June 1445 (PCC 32 Luffenam).

PREBENDARIES OF WARTHACWM

Richard Bermyngham ?–1394.
Vac. this preb. before 26 May 1394 (*CPR. 1391–1396* p. 412).

Nicholas Bubwith 1394–1396.
Royal gr. 26 May 1394 (*CPR. 1391–1396* p. 412). Res. before 22 June 1396 (*CPR. 1396–1399* p. 1).

---

[1] Passemer must have been rector of the ch. of St Nicholas, Glam., 6 miles from Cardiff and in Llandaff dioc., as there is no ch. of St Nicholas within Llandaff. The endowment of the preb. of St Nicholas in Llandaff cath. came from this ch. and it seems probable that the rectors held the preb.

Patrick atte Wode 1396-?
Royal gr. 22 June 1396 (*CPR. 1396-1399* p. 1).

Roger Gruffudd 1535.
Occ. 1535 (*Valor* IV 347).

UNIDENTIFIED PREBENDARIES

M. Thomas de Neville 1322.
Occ. 11 June 1322 (*CPL.* II 221).

William de Herlaston 1323, 1330.
Occ. as preb. 7 July 1323 (P.R.O., C 84/20/20). Occ. as can. 3 Feb. 1330 (*CPL.* II 305).

M. Edmund de Meopham D.Th. 1327.
Occ. 14 July 1327 (*CPL.* II 273).

Otto de Sapiti 1328.
Occ. 11 Oct. 1328 (*CPL.* II 282).

John de Coventry 1343-?
Prov. 22 Oct. 1343 (*CPP.* I 24).

M. Richard de Turville Sch.Th. 1346.
Occ. 7 Aug. 1346 (*CPL.* III 238).

Peter de Gildesburgh 1349.
Occ. 28 May 1349 (*CPL.* III 314).

William de Wykeham 1361.
Occ. 20 Jan. 1361 (*CPP.* I 363).

M. Henry Despenser B.C.L. 1366.
Occ. 17 Oct. 1366 (*Reg. Langham* p. 61). ? Held preb. until 1370 when bp. of Norwich. Succeeded by Richard de Croxton (see below).

Richard de Croxton ?-1380.
Exch. preb. vac. by Henry Despenser (see above) and preb. of Axford, Salisbury, with Thomas Banastre of Eltisley for preb. of Dunham and Newport, Lincoln, 18/22 Nov. 1380 (Lincoln, Reg. X (Buckingham) ff. 108b-109; Salis., Reg. Erghum f. 51b; see below).[1]

M. Thomas Banastre of Eltisley B.Cn. & C.L. 1380-1385.
By exch. with Richard de Croxton for preb. of Dunham and Newport, Lincoln, 18/22 Nov. 1380 (Lincoln, Reg. X (Buckingham) ff. 108b-109; Salis., Reg. Erghum f. 51b; see above). Exch. preb. and ch. of Eltisley, Cambs., with John de Barton for a preb. in Exeter cath., 7/17 Dec. 1385 (Exeter Chapter Library, Dean and Chapter MS. 3550 f. 14/17; Ely, Reg. Arundell f. 54; see below).

M. John de Barton 1385-?
By exch. with Thomas Banastre of Eltisley for a preb. in Exeter cath., 7/17 Dec. 1385 (Exeter Chapter Library, Dean and Chapter MS. 3550 f. 14/17; Ely, Reg. Arundell f. 54; see above).

---

[1] The Llandaff exch. is not included in the Salis. reg.

Thomas de Alston ?–1392/3.

D. as preb. Dec. 1392/Feb. 1393 (PCC 7 Rous; *CPR. 1391–1396* p. 241). Succeeded by Thomas Sparkeford (see below).

M. **Thomas Sparkeford** 1393–1396.

Royal gr. 3 March 1393 of preb. vac. by Thomas de Alston (*CPR. 1391–1396* p. 241; see above). Bp. of Waterford and Lismore 1396.

Thomas Newenham ?–1394.

D. as preb. before 25 May 1394 (*CPR. 1391–1396* p. 416). Succeeded by John de Lincoln (see below).

M. **John de Lincoln** Sch.Cn.L. 1394–?

Royal gr. 25 May 1394 of preb. vac. by Thomas Newenham (*CPR. 1391–1396* p. 416; see above).

M. **William Croucheston** D.C.L. 1422.

Occ. 13 Aug. 1422 (*CPL.* VII 246–7).

M. **David Nuporte** D.Cn.L. 1428.

Occ. 7 Apr. 1428 (*CPL.* VIII 27).

David Newcastle 1438.

Occ. 28 Dec. 1438 (*CPL.* IX 5).

John Sadyngton 1441.

Occ. 17 Feb. 1441 (*Reg. Chichele* I 125).

M. **John Wynter** ?–1478.

D. as preb. before 2 May 1478 (*CPR. 1476–1485* p. 98). Succeeded by John Kyrkeby (see below).

John Kyrkeby 1478–?

Royal gr. 2 May 1478 of preb. vac. by John Wynter (*CPR. 1476–1485* p. 98; see above).

M. **Thomas Fysshewyke** B.Cn.L. ?–1508.

D. as preb. 22 Aug./11 Sept. 1508 (PCC 7 Bennett).

M. **William Clerk** ?–1537.

Occ. 1535 (*Valor* IV 347). Res. by 24 Jan. 1537[1] (*L. & P.* XII i No. 311 (20)). Succeeded by John Farewell (see below).

M. **William Hywel** 1535.

Occ. 1535 (*Valor* IV 347).

M. **William Johns** 1535.

Occ. 1535 (*Valor* IV 347).

M. **Gruffudd Leyshon** D.C.L. 1535.

Occ. 1535 (*Valor* IV 348).

M. — **Mayo** 1535.

Occ. 1535 (*Valor* IV 348).

M. **John Farewell** M.A. 1537–?

Royal gr. 24 Jan. 1537 to preb. vac. by William Clerk[1] (*L. & P.* XII i No. 311 (20); see above).

---

[1] The preb. was called 'preb. of a fourth part of the tithes of corn' ('decimarum garbarum cursalium') (*L. & P.* XII i No. 311 (20)).

CANONS WITH EXPECTATION OF PREBENDS

M. Richard de Stoke D.C.L. 1317–?
Prov. 11 July 1317 and 11 July 1318 (*CPL*. II 159, 173). Occ. 9 Oct. 1338 (*Memorials of Llandaff* p. 331).

Vincent de Bergevenny 1327–?
Prov. 14 July 1327 (*CPL*. II 259).

Thomas Skydemor 1330–?
Prov. 11 Apr. 1330 (*CPL*. II 308).

Richard de Clifford 1343–?
Prov. 18 July 1343 (*CPL*. III 101).

Thomas Enham 1347–?
Prov. 22 July 1347 (*CPL*. III 257). Occ. 1 Feb. 1350 (*ibid*. p. 316).

Thomas de Castrogodrici 1348–?
Prov. 19 May 1348 (*CPL*. III 279).

M. Robert de Elteslee B.C.L. 1363–?
Prov. 27 June 1363 (*CPP*. I 436). Occ. July 1366 (*Reg. Langham* p. 105).

M. Thomas de Stratford Lic.Cn.L., B.C.L. 1366.
Occ. Sept. 1366 (*Reg. Langham* p. 36).

M. John Landreyn B.Th., B.M. 1366.
Occ. 16 Oct. 1366 (Lincoln, Reg. XII (Buckingham) f. 46b).

Dafydd ap Hywel 1398–?
Mand. adm. 22 March 1398 if found fit in Latin (*CPL*. V 99–100).

CANONS OF LLANDAFF

M. John de Middleton 1324, 1328.
Occ. 27 Oct. 1324 (Lamb., Reg. Reynolds f. 165b). Occ. June 1328 (Nat. Libr. Wales, MS. 17110 E f. 117).

John de Miltone 1338.
Occ. 9 Oct. 1338 (*Memorials of Llandaff* p. 331).

Gilbert de Wygetoune 1338.
Occ. 9 Oct. 1338 (*Memorials of Llandaff* p. 331).

M. Richard de Haverisham B.C.L. 1342, 1347.
Occ. 28 Apr. 1342 (*CPL*. II 60). Occ. 20 Jan. 1347 (*Black Prince's Reg*. I 42).

Geoffrey de Cornasano 1343–1353.
Prov. 8 Aug. 1343 (*CPL*. II 135). Exch. canonry with Henry de Exon for a canonry with reservn. of preb. in Lanchester colleg. ch., co. Dur., 12 March 1353 (*ibid*. p. 482; see below p. 33).

William de Wygeton 1347.
Occ. 20 Jan. 1347 (*Black Prince's Reg*. I 42).

Henry de Exon 1353-?
By exch. with Geoffrey de Cornasano for a canonry with reservn. of preb. in Lanchester colleg. ch., co. Dur., 12 March 1353 (*CPL*. II 482; see above p. 32).

M. Roger Croke 1385, 1397.
Occ. 22 Jan. 1385 (*Memorials of Llandaff* p. 337). Occ. 20 Feb. 1397 (*Cartae et Munimenta de Glamorgan* IV 1426).

M. Richard de Suthbury 1385.
Occ. 22 Jan. 1385 (*Memorials of Llandaff* p. 337).

Thomas Orewelle 1393.
Occ. 10 June 1393 (PCC 3 Rous).

Henry Ware 1394, 1414.
Occ. 5 May 1394 (*CPL*. IV 472). Occ. 10 Jan. 1414 (*Foedera* IV ii 60-1). ? Held canonry until 1418 when bp. of Chichester.

John Cors 1397.
Occ. 20 Feb. 1397 (*Cartae et Munimenta de Glamorgan* IV 1427).

M. John Traharn B.Cn. & C.L. 1400.
Occ. 1 May 1400 (*CPL*. V 273).

John Davy 1423, 1425.
Occ. 2 and 6 July 1423 (*Reg. Chichele* II 247-9). Occ. 10 July 1425 (*CPR. 1422-1429* pp. 289-90).

Dafydd Llywellyn 1473.
Occ. 18 Oct. 1473 (*Cartae et Munimenta de Glamorgan* V 1700-1).

William ap John 1476, 1477.
Occ. 3 June 1476 (*CPL*. XIII ii 508). Occ. 5 Jan. 1477 (*ibid*. p. 544).

M. William Sherwood D.Th. 1479.
Occ. 9 Jan. 1479 (*CPL*. XIII i 210).

Thomas Gwynllwg 1487.
Occ. 26 Sept. 1487 (*Cartae et Munimenta de Glamorgan* V 1735).

Matthew David 1535.
Occ. 1535 (*Valor* IV 347).

William Davy 1535.
Occ. 1535 (*Valor* IV 347).

William Edmund 1535.
Occ. 1535 (*Valor* IV 347).

John Eton 1535.
Occ. 1535 (*Valor* IV 347).

Thomas Gethyn 1535.
Occ. 1535 (*Valor* IV 347).

John Goch 1535.
Occ. 1535 (*Valor* IV 347).

Thomas Hywel 1535.
Occ. 1535 (*Valor* IV 347).

John Jankyns 1535.
Occ. 1535 (*Valor* IV 347).

M. **John Jevans** 1535.
    Occ. 1535 (*Valor* IV 347).

M. **William Mather** 1535.
    Occ. 1535 (*Valor* IV 347).

Thomas Morgan 1535.
    Occ. 1535 (*Valor* IV 347).

Hugh Philip 1535.
    Occ. 1535 (*Valor* IV 347).

William Raglan 1535.
    Occ. 1535 (*Valor* IV 347).

Thomas Robert 1535.
    Occ. 1535 (*Valor* IV 347).

Richard Sais 1535.
    Occ. 1535 (*Valor* IV 347).

— **Sawndyr** 1535.
    Occ. 1535 (*Valor* IV 347).

John Synger 1535.
    Occ. 1535 (*Valor* IV 347).

Morgan Thomas 1535.
    Occ. 1535 (*Valor* IV 347).

Lewis Which 1535.
    Occ. 1535 (*Valor* IV 347).

St Asaph 1300-1541

MANUSCRIPT MATERIAL

National Library of Wales, Aberystwyth

Additional MS. 7011 D.	St Asaph Llyfr Côch, sixteenth-century transcript.
SA/BR/1, 2.	Registers of bps., 1536–58, 1558–1595.
SA/MB/14.	St Asaph Memorandum Book.

Canterbury Cathedral Library

Registers A, Q, S, T.

Lambeth Palace Library

The registers of the archbishops of Canterbury from Reynolds to Cranmer, 1314–1555.

Somerset House

PCC: Registers of wills proved in the prerogative court of Canterbury.

M. Llywellyn ab Ynyr *or* **de Bromfield** 1293–1314.

Lic. el. gr. 23 Feb. 1293 (*CPR. 1292–1301* p. 5). El. 9 March (Cant., Reg. A f. 313/357). Royal assent sought 18 Apr. (P.R.O., C 84/11/14), gr. 6 May (*CPR. 1292–1301* p. 12). El. conf. by prior of Canterbury 8 May (Cant., Reg. Q f. 50/65). Temps. 13 May (*CPR. 1292–1301* p. 15). Cons. 17 May at Canterbury (Cant., Reg. A f. 313/357). D. before 25 Jan. 1314 (P.R.O., C 84/18/9).

M. Dafydd ap Bleddyn 1314–1345.

Lic. el. sought 25 Jan. 1314 (P.R.O., C 84/18/9). El. 23 June (*Brut y Tywysogyon* p. 123). Lic. el. gr. 18 July (*CPR. 1313–1317* p. 160). Royal assent 7 Sept. (*ibid.* p. 170). Mand. by abp. 22 Sept. to examine el. (Lamb., Reg. Reynolds f. 111). Temps. 1 Nov. (*CPR. 1313–1317* p. 190). Cons. 12/13 Jan. 1315 (Cant., Reg. A f. 313/357; *Reg. S. de Gandavo*, ed. C. T. Flower and M. C. B. Dawes (Canterbury and York Soc., xl, xli) 1 511). D. before 9 Oct. 1345 (*CCR. 1343–1346* p. 656).

[John de Lincoln O.P. 1345.]
[M. Griffin Trefor D.Cn.L. 1345.]
M. John Trefor B.Th. 1346–1357.

K. requested chapt. at St Asaph to el. Lincoln, his confessor, as bp. 9 Oct. 1345 (*CCR. 1343–1346* p. 656). Richard de Stafford, official of the Prince of Wales, came to Flint 19 Oct., met four canons of St Asaph and instructed them to meet him 20 Oct. for discussion about el. (*Cal. Anct. Correspondence* pp. 241–2). Letter from Prince of Wales read to canons s.d., canons stated that they would not have an Englishman as bp. (*ibid.*). Report by Richard de Stafford 6 Nov. that chapt. at St Asaph had held el. (*ibid.*). El. of Griffin Trefor by chapt. announced 24 Nov. (*ibid.* p. 240). El. not accepted, bpc. said to be vac. 12 Feb. 1346 (*CCR. 1346–1349* p. 46). John Trefor prov. n.d., but received papal mand. 24 July instructing him to depart to dioc. of St Asaph after cons. by bp. of Ostia (*CPL.* III 229). Temps. 21 Sept. (*Black Prince's Reg.* I 19). Profession to abp. of Canterbury 24 March 1353 (Cant., Reg. A f. 313b/357b). D. before 9 Feb. 1357 (*Black Prince's Reg.* III 234).

[William de Spridlington 1357.]
M. Llywellyn ap Madog ab Elis 1357–1375.

El. of Spridlington requested n.d. by the Prince of Wales (*Williams* p. 126). Llywellyn el. by chapt. n.d., but prov. 19 July 1357 and el. by chapt. annulled (Lamb., Reg. Islip f. 218). Spir. 30 Oct. (*ibid.*). Cons. n.d. at Rome (*R.S.A.*). Mand. 9 Aug. 1359 to make profession to abp. (Lamb., Reg. Islip f. 152b). Profession to abp. 16 May 1360 (*ibid.* f. 159b). D. before 24 Nov. 1375 (Lamb., Reg. Sudbury ff. 23–23b).

William de Spridlington (again) 1376–1382.

Prov. 4 Feb. 1376 (Lamb., Reg. Sudbury f. 18). Profession to abp. 29 Apr. (*ibid.*). Spir. s.d. (*ibid.*). Cons. by abp. 25 May (*ibid.* f. 20). D. 9 Apr. 1382 (Lamb., Reg. Courtenay f. 313).

M. Lawrence Child O.S.B., Lic.Cn.L. 1382–1389.

Lic. el. gr. 19 May 1382 (*CPR. 1381–1385* p. 115). Prov. 18 June (Lamb., Reg. Courtenay f. 315b). Cons. in Aug. (*R.S.A.*). Spir. 2 Oct. (Lamb., Reg. Courtenay f. 316). Temps. 20 Oct. (*CPR. 1381–1385* p. 173). D. 20 Dec. 1389 (Lamb., Reg. Courtenay f. 173).

[M. **John Trefor** D.Cn. & C.L. 1390.]

M. Alexander Bache O.P., D.Th. 1390–1394.

Lic. el. sought 4 Jan. 1390 (P.R.O., C 84/34/37). Lic. el. gr. 13 Jan. (*CPR. 1388–1392* p. 176). Trefor el. n.d., k. gr. lic. 27 Feb. to go to curia for cons. unless Bache had been already prov. (*ibid.* p. 223). Bache prov. at k's request 28 Feb. (Lamb., Reg. Courtenay ff. 326–326b). Spir. 6 Apr. (*ibid.* f. 173). Temps. 28 Apr. (*CPR. 1388–1392* p. 247). Cons. 8 May (*R.S.A.*). D. 13/15 Sept. 1394 (PCC 4 Rous).

M. John Trefor D.Cn. & C.L. (again) 1394–?, ?–1410.

Lic. el. gr. 15 Sept. 1394 (*CPR. 1391–1396* p. 482). El. 3 Oct. (P.R.O., C 84/3/10). Prov. 21 Oct. (*CPL.* IV 481). Royal lic. to accept bpc. to which prov. 9 Apr. 1395 (*CPR. 1391–1396* p. 563). Assent of parliament s.d. (*Rot. Parl.* III 407). Temps. 6 July (*CPR. 1391–1396* p. 593). Cons. at Rome n.d. (*R.S.A.*). Trans. to St Andrews[1] c. 1408 (*Eubel* I 89 n. 10), spir. of St Asaph assigned to Thomas, abbot of Shrewsbury, 1408 (Lamb., Reg. Arundell I f. 451). Trefor restored to bpc. of St Asaph before 24 May 1410 (*CPL.* VI 207). Pope gr. Trefor s.d. four or more benefices in dioc. of Rheims, France, as he had received no money from bpc. for several years because of divers troubles in Wales (*ibid.*). D. before 16 July (*ibid.* pp. 198–9).

Robert of Lancaster O.Cist. 1410–1433.

Prov. 16 July 1410 (*CPL.* VI 198–9). Cons. 28 June 1411 by abp. at Lincoln (Lamb., Reg. Arundell II f. 130b). Profession and spir. s.d. (*ibid.*). D. 26 March 1433 (P.R.O., C 84/42/46).

M. John Lowe O.F.S.A., D.Th. 1433–1444.

Lic. el. sought 6 Apr. 1433 (P.R.O., C 84/42/46). Lic. el. gr. 26 Apr. (*CPR. 1429–1436* p. 262). Prov. 17 Aug. (*Reg. Chichele* I 117). Temps. 17 Oct. (*CPR. 1429–1436* p. 321). Lic. *alibi cons.* 19 Oct. (Cant., Reg. S f. 126/116). Mand. to restore spir. 21 Oct. (*Reg. Chichele* I 117–18). Trans. to Rochester 1444.

M. Reginald Pecock D.Th. 1444–1450.

Prov. 22 Apr. 1444 (Lamb., Reg. Stafford ff. 15–15b). Temps. 8 June (*CPR. 1441–1446* p. 272). Cons. 14 June by abp. at Croydon, Surr. (Lamb., Reg. Stafford f. 15). Profession to abp. and spir. s.d. (*ibid.* ff. 15–15b). Trans. to Chichester 1450.

M. Thomas Bird O.P., D.Th. 1450–?

Prov. 27 March 1450 (*CPL.* X 509). Cons. probably 14 Feb. 1451 (*R.S.A.*). Depriv. c. 1463—temps. then in k's hands (*Reg. Bourgchier* p. 270). Custody of temps. gr. to Richard Caunton and James Stanley 11 March and 30 June 1465 (*CPR. 1461–1467* pp. 428–9, 467).

---

[1] Trefor's trans. to St Andrews can be considered a banishment from Wales as a result of his part in Owain Glyn Dŵr's rebellion (*Williams* pp. 223–5). Alexander de Neville abp. of York, and Thomas Arundell abp. of Canterbury had similarly been exiled there in 1388 and 1397 after deposition and attainder (Le Neve, *Fasti, 1300–1541*, rev. ed., VI 4, IV 4). It is difficult to estimate how long Trefor was absent from St Asaph, as he was unable to obtain possession of St Andrews (*Eubel* I 89 n. 10), but nothing is heard of him until 24 May 1410 when a papal mandate was addressed to him as bp. of St Asaph (*CPL.* VI 207). But he is said to have died 10 Apr. (*R.S.A.*). His place of residence between 1408 and his d. in 1410 is unknown. He could have been at the papal ct. or in hiding in Wales, or even in Scotland, as he had previously been employed as ambassador there by Richard II (*Williams* p. 219).

M. **Richard Redman** O.Prem., M.A. Abbot of Shap. 1471–1495.

Lic. *alibi cons.* 13 Oct. 1471 (Cant., Reg. S f. 255).[1] Prov. 17 Aug. 1472 (*CPL.* XIII i 316). Trans. to Exeter 1495.

M. **Michael Diacre** O.S.B., D.Th. 1496–1500.

Lic. *alibi cons.* 11 Jan. 1496 (Cant., Reg. S f. 404b). Cons. in England before 1 Feb., then called bp., not bp. el. (*R.S.A.*; *CPR. 1494–1509* p. 46). D. before 10 March 1500 (Cant., Reg. S ff. 433–433b).

Dafydd ab Ieuan ab Iorwerth O.Cist. 1500–1503.

Lic. *alibi cons.* 10 March 1500 (Cant., Reg. S ff. 433–433b). Cons. by abp. 26 Apr. (*R.S.A.*). D. before 18 Dec. 1503 (Lamb., Reg. Warham I f. 3).

M. **Dafydd ab Owain** O.Cist., D.Cn.L. 1503–1513.

Prov. 18 Dec. 1503 (Lamb., Reg. Warham I f. 3). Lic. *alibi cons.* 31 Jan. 1504 (Cant., Reg. T ff. 442–442b). Cons. in Feb. (*R.S.A.*). D. 11/12 Feb. 1513 (PCC 23 Fetiplace; Lamb., Reg. Warham II ff. 268–268b).

M. **Edmund Birkhead** O.F.M., D.Th. 1513–1518.

Prov. 15 Apr. 1513 (Lamb., Reg. Warham I f. 16). Lic. *alibi cons.* 27 May (*ibid.* ff. 16–16b). Cons. by abp. at Lambeth 29 May (*ibid.* f. 16b). Profession to abp. s.d. (*ibid.*). D. before 9 Apr. 1518 (*ibid.* II ff. 269b–270).

M. **Henry Standish** O.F.M., D.Th. 1518–1535.

[**William Bolton** O.Can.S.A. Prior of St Bartholomew's, Smithfield. 1518.]

Standish nominated by k. 12 Apr. 1518 (*L. & P.* II ii No. 4074). Wolsey had nominated Bolton n.d. (*ibid.* No. 4083). K. promised 14 Apr. that would give some small preferment to Bolton because had already promised bpc. to Standish (*ibid.*). Standish prov. 28/29 May (Lamb., Reg. Warham I ff. 20b–21). Lic. *alibi cons.* 8 July (*ibid.* f. 21). Cons. 11 July by abp. at Otford, Kent (*ibid.* ff. 21–21b). Mand. to restore spir. 12 July (*ibid.* f. 21b). D. 9 July 1535 (Lamb., Reg. Cranmer f. 181).

[M. **Fouke Salisbury** M.A. 1535.]

M. **William Barlow** O.Can.S.A., D.Th. 1536.

Salisbury sent petition 10 July 1535 to Thomas Cromwell that might be gr. bpc. (*L. & P.* VIII No. 1014). Not gr. as chapt. received lic. el. 7 Jan. 1536 (*ibid.* x No. 226 (4)). Barlow el. 16 Jan. (Lamb., Reg. Cranmer f. 181b). Royal assent 20/22 Feb. (*ibid.* f. 180b; *L. & P.* x No. 392 (45)). Conf. by abp. 23 Feb. (Lamb., Reg. Cranmer ff. 182b–183). Bp. of St Davids, el. 10 Apr.

M. **Robert Wharton** *or* **Parfew** O.Clun., B.Th. 1536–1554.

Lic. el. gr. 29 May 1536 (*L. & P.* x No. 1015 (36)). El. 8 June (Lamb., Reg. Cranmer f. 196). Royal assent 24 June (*L. & P.* x No. 1256 (47)). Assent of abp. 26 June (Lamb., Reg. Cranmer ff. 193b–194). Cons. 2 July by abp. at Lambeth (*ibid.* f. 197). Temps. 21 July (*L. & P.* XI No. 202 (42)). Bp. of Hereford 1554.

---

[1] Redman had papal lic. to retain the abbey of Shap and one other benefice *in commendam* with the bpc. 17 Aug. 1472 (*CPL.* XIII i 316) and again 10 June 1485 (*ibid.* XIV 13).

DEANS OF ST ASAPH

Einion 1301, 1314.
Occ. Sept. 1301 (*Thomas* I 317).[1] Occ. 4 July 1314 (Lamb., Reg. Reynolds f. 56b).

Bleddyn ab Einion 1345.
Occ. 12 March 1345 (*Cal. Anct. Correspondence* p. 227).

Benedict 1345.
Occ. 24 Nov. 1345 (*Cal. Anct. Correspondence* p. 240).

M. Llywellyn ap Madog ab Elis ?–1357.
Res. deanery 19 July 1357 when prov. to bpc. of St Asaph (Lamb., Reg. Islip f. 218).

M. Benedict de Montealto[2] *or* **Benet ab Iorwerth** Sch.Cn.L., B.C.L. 1357–1358.
Robert de Walsham 1357–?
Deanery reserved for Benedict de Montealto 2 Aug. 1357 (*CPL.* III 581). Prov. before 3 Sept. (*CPP.* I 301). Walsham presented to abp. by the Prince of Wales as dn. 17 Oct. (*Black Prince's Reg.* III 281). Mand. by abp. to adm. 20 Oct. (Lamb., Reg. Islip f. 279). Mand. 24 Nov. to escheator for Cheshire and Flint to seize Benet ab Iorwerth who had procured the deanery by papal prov. and to imprison him (*Black Prince's Reg.* III 282). Benet ab Iorwerth still in possession of the deanery 10 Dec. as second mand. sent by the Prince of Wales to seize and imprison him (*ibid.* p. 289). Occ. as dn. 18 Dec. (*ibid.* p. 290). Captured by 6 Feb. 1358 as order sent then to Constable of Chester castle 'to guard the said Benet in irons', but 'in a decent chamber within the castle' and to allow him 'the comfort of fire and other necessaries' (*ibid.* p. 291).

Richard de Spridlington 1366.
Occ. 23 Sept. 1366 (Lincoln, Reg. XII (Buckingham) f. 446).

William de Spridlington ?–1376.
Occ. 11 June 1375 (*Cat. Anct. Deeds* II 373). Bp. of St Asaph 1376.[3]

David de Calvyley 1380, 1381.
Estate ratif. 19 Dec. 1380 (*CPR. 1377–1381* p. 583). Occ. 30 March 1381 (Lichfield, Reg. IV (Stretton) f. 124b).

Dafydd Fychan ap Dafydd 1385–1386.
Hywel ap Madog ap Cyffin 1386, 1401.
Hugh Cotyngham 1393.
Royal gr. to Fychan 25 Aug. 1385 (*CPR. 1385–1389* p. 15). Estate of Hywel ratif. 11 May 1386 (*ibid.* p. 145). Gr. to Fychan revoked 16 Oct. as said to have obtained deanery by fraud, by falsely asserting that it was then vac. (*ibid.* p. 230). Hywel occ. 20 Dec. 1389 (Lamb., Reg. Courtenay f. 173). Estate of Cotyngham ratif. 4 Sept. 1393 (*CPR. 1391–1396* p. 327). Hywel had regained possession of the deanery by 1394 as letter sent that year from the Earl of Arundel and Surrey to abp. of York, with request that he should show favour to Hywel, because Morgan the Young, sheriff of Flint, was trying to oust him from the deanery for the benefit of his own son (*Anglo-Norman*

---

[1] 'Anianus decanus dedit 5 marcas p'sbytero in Eccl. Asaph serviend' ex camera sua et successoribus suis decanis, terminis infra scriptis solvendas . . . Dat . . . die Dom. p' xim' post Fest Beati Matt. A.D. 1301 [i.e. 24 Sept.].—*Old MS. Bk.*'
[2] Benedict de Montealto (of Mold, Flints.) can be identified with Benet ab Iorwerth who is also called Benet de Mohaut (Mold) (*Black Prince's Reg.* III 333–4).
[3] There is no evidence that Alan de Stokes held the deanery 1376 as stated by Le Neve-Hardy.

Letters and Petitions, ed. M. D. Legge (Oxford, 1941) pp. 76–8). Royal pardon gr. to Hywel 6 May 1401 (*CPR. 1399–1401* p. 452). Probably held deanery until d., c. 1402 (*CPL.* IV 420; *Emden, Reg. Ox.* II 1067).

M. **Richard Courtenay** B.C.L. 1402–?
Royal gr. 16 May 1402 (*CPR. 1401–1405* p. 93). Adm. 4 June (Lamb., Reg. Arundell I ff. 110–110b).

Hugh Holbache 1404, 1414.
Estate ratif. 3 Feb. 1404 (*CPR. 1401–1405* p. 349). Occ. 18 March 1414 (*CPL.* VI 402). ? Held deanery until d., 1417 (*Emden, Reg. Ox.* II 945).

M. **Richard Leyot** D.C.L. 1419, 1420.
Occ. 18 March 1419 (*Foedera* IV iii 101). Occ. 4 March 1420 (*CPL.* VII 146).

John Halle ?–1425.
Exch. deanery with Ralph Wellys for ch. of Alrewas, Staffs., 2 March 1425 (Lichfield, Reg. IX (Heyworth) f. 51b).

Ralph Wellys 1425–?
By exch. March 1425.

M. **John Blodwel** B.C.L. 1429, 1433.
Occ. 29 Oct. 1429 (*CPL.* VIII 148–9). Occ. 6 Apr. 1433 (P.R.O., C 84/42/46).

M. **Dafydd Blodwel** Lic.C.L. ?–1461.
Occ. 18 March 1455 (*CPL.* XI 22). Estate ratif. 29 Oct. 1459 (*CPR. 1452–1461* p. 464). D. by Aug. 1461 (*Emden, Reg. Camb.* p. 66).

M. **John Tapton** Sch.Th. 1461–?
Royal gr. 18 Aug. 1461 (*CPR. 1461–1467* p. 47). Coll. by abp. of Canterbury 27 Jan. 1463 (*Reg. Bourgchier* p. 270).

M. **Fouke Salisbury** ?–1543.
Occ. 3 Oct. 1475 (*CPL.* XIII ii 473). Occ. 1529 (*L. & P.* IV iii No. 6047 p. 2701). D. before 3 Nov. 1543 (Nat. Libr. Wales, SA/BR/I f. 6b).

CHANCELLORS OF ST ASAPH

Note : The prebend of Llannefydd was attached to the chancellorship.

Reginald de Hulton 1382, 1386.
John de Excestre 1385–1386.
Estate of Hulton ratif. as preb. of Llannefydd 13 Feb. 1382 (*CPR. 1381–1385* p. 96). Displaced by royal gr. of preb. to Excestre 28 Aug. 1385 (*CPR. 1385–1389* p. 14). Gr. revoked 24 May 1386 and Hulton restored to possession s.d. (*ibid.* p. 159).

John Carp 1399.
Estate ratif. as preb. of Llannefydd 28 Oct. 1399 (*CPR. 1399–1401* p. 25).

M. **Richard Standish** B.A. 1535.
Occ. 1535 (*Valor* IV 435).

PRECENTORS OF ST ASAPH

Note: The prebend of Faenol was attached to the precentorship.

Robert de Stretton 1344/57.
Royal gr. by the Prince of Wales 25 Jan. 1344/57 of preb. called 'Dymmerghion'[1] (*Cal. Anct. Correspondence* p. 238).

Gruffudd ab Ieuan Grath 1393.
Estate ratif. as preb. 'Thome presbiteri'[2] 28 June 1393 (*CPR. 1391-1396* p. 309).

John ap Rhys ap Roppert ?-1404.
D. as preb. and precentor before 17 March 1404 (*CPL.* v 579).

M. **John ap Hywel ap Brython D.Th. ?-1538.**
Occ. 1535 (*Valor* IV 435). D. before 9 Apr. 1538 (Nat. Libr. Wales, SA/BR/1 f. 5).

M. **Maurice Byrchynshawe M.A. 1538-?**
Coll. 9 Apr. 1538 (Nat. Libr. Wales, SA/BR/1 f. 5). Occ. 1559/60 (*Thomas* I 290) —in a return of bp. Richard Davies (1559-1561).

TREASURERS OF ST ASAPH

Note: The prebend of Meliden was attached to the treasurership.

Hugh le Yonge 1366.
Prov. to canonry with reservn. of preb. 8 Feb. 1355 (*CPL.* III 544). Occ. as preb. of Meliden 29 Nov. 1366 (*Reg. Langham* p. 89).

M. **John Prophete 1395.**
Estate ratif. 15 May 1395 (*CPR. 1391-1396* p. 569). ? Held preb. of Meliden 24 Sept. 1402 when occ. as unnamed preb. (*CPL.* IV 354).

M. **Thomas Felde ?-1404.**
Occ. 29 Sept. 1403 (*CPL.* v 537). Exch. preb. of Meliden with John Trefnant for preb. of Withington Parva, Hereford, 6 Jan. 1404 (Hereford, Reg. Trefnant f. 53).

M. **John Trefnant** *or* **ap Hywel 1404-?**
By exch. Jan. 1404.

Robert Gowe 1407-?
Royal gr. 29 May 1407 (*CPR. 1405-1408* p. 325).

William Tyrell 1413-?
Royal gr. 15 May 1413 (*CPR. 1413-1416* p. 15).

M. **Adam Moleyns D.C.L. ?-1441.**
Occ. as unnamed preb. 5 Nov. 1439 (*CPL.* IX 84-5). Exch. preb. of Meliden and treasurership with William Hoper for ch. of St Michael Crooked Lane, London, 27 Nov. 1441 (*Reg. Chichele* I 305).

[1] This is the older form of the place name Tremeirchion, Flints. (*Thomas* I 400). The ch. of Tremeirchion formed part of the endowment of the preb. of Faenol (*Valor* IV 440).

[2] Gruffudd ab Ieuan Grath must have held the precentorship as the 'canonry of Thomas the priest' was the name given to a subdivision of the township of Faenol which was appropriated to the precentorship. The canonry was included under that dignity in the *Taxatio* of 1291: 'Canonia Thome Presbyteri in Parochia ipsius Ecclesiae' (Faenol) (*Thomas* I 422).

M. William Hoper D.Cn. & C.L. 1441–?
By exch. Nov. 1441. ? Held preb. and treasurership until d., by May 1454 (*Emden, Reg. Ox.* II 959).

Roger Chesshyre 1465.
Estate ratif. 6 July 1465 (*CPR. 1461–1467* p. 444).

Robert Sharpuls ?–1476.
Exch. preb. of Meliden with Edmund Chaterton for mastership of St Leonard's hospital, York, 28 May 1476 (*CPR. 1467–1477* p. 585).

M. Edmund Chaterton 1476–?
By exch. May 1476.

Gregory Flynt 1513.
Occ. 11 Feb. 1513 (PCC 23 Fetiplace).

Christopher Wellisford 1535.
Occ. as preb. of Meliden 1535 (*Valor* IV 436).

ARCHDEACONS OF ST ASAPH

Gruffudd 1293, 1306.[1]
Occ. 1 May 1293 (Cant., Reg. Q f. 14/4). Occ. 5 Oct. 1306 (Nat. Libr. Wales, Add. MS. 7011 D p. 3).

Llywellyn ap Hwfa ?–1330.
'L' occ. 1307 (*Rot. Parl.* I 190). Llywellyn ap Hwfa d. as archdcn. after 24 June 1330 (*Brut y Tywysogyon* p. 126).

M. Llywellyn ap Madog ab Elis 1331.
Occ. 1331 (Worcester, Reg. Orleton II f. 11b).

M. Ithel ap Robert B.C.L. ?–1402.
M. Thomas Rushooke O.P., M.Th. 1382–1383.
Thomas Keler 1390.
Ithel ap Robert occ. 6 Oct. 1371 (Lamb., Reg. Wittlesey f. 136). Royal gr. to Rushooke 9 June 1382 (*CPR. 1381–1385* p. 131). Bp. of Llandaff 1383. Ithel ap Robert obtained possession of archdcnry again, occ. 20 Sept. 1390 (*CPL.* IV 328). Thomas Keler occ. as rector of Dyserth, Flints.[2] 24 Nov. (*ibid.* p. 329). He was then gr. lic. to be absent from his benefice for life if necessary and was therefore probably unaware of the litigation over the archdcnry. Ithel ap Robert d. before 5 Feb. 1402 (*ibid.* V 483)[3] —called Ippart ap Robert.

---

[1] William de Testa was said by Le Neve-Hardy to have been archdcn. of St Asaph 1306. There has been confusion between the Latin form for St Asaph, 'Assavensis', and 'Aranensis', the Latin for Aran. Testa at this time held the archdcnry of Aran, in the ch. of St Bertrand de Comminges, situated in the Val d'Aran, now in Spain, but which was a member of the dioc. of Comminges until the French Revolution (*Reg. of W. Greenfield*, ed. W. Brown and A. H. Thompson (Surtees Soc., 1931–8) I 22 n. 2).

[2] The ch. of Dyserth formed part of the endowment of the archdcnry (*Valor* IV 435; *Thomas* I 400). The estate of Iorwerth ap Rhys was ratif. as 'parson' of Dyserth 30 Nov. 1391 (*CPR. 1388–1392* p. 512) but he probably held the vicarage and not the rectory. John Moel was presented to the ch. of Dyserth 30 Oct. 1407 (*CPR. 1405–1408* p. 366) and could possibly have been archdcn.

[3] There is no evidence that Dafydd Fychan ap Dafydd was archdcn. of St Asaph 1386 or that Griffin le Yonge was archdcn. in 1398, 1403 and 1406 as stated by Le Neve-Hardy.

M. Edward Trefor 1425.
    Occ. 30 June 1425 (*CPL.* VII 378).

M. Dafydd Nant D.Cn. & C.L. 1438.
    Occ. 17 May 1438 (*CPL.* VIII 392).

M. John Tubney ?–1457.
    Occ. 16 Dec. 1444 (*Registrum Roffense*, ed. J. Thorpe (London, 1769) p. 510). D. before 10 June 1457 (Rochester, Reg. Lowe f. 229).[1]

    Peter Conway ?–1532.
    Occ. 1509/10 (*L. & P.* I i No. 438 (3) p. 246). D. before 17 July 1532 (PCC 16 Thower).

    Richard Shelton 1535.
    Occ. 1535 (*Valor* IV 434).

PREBENDARIES OF FAENOL

The prebend of Faenol was attached to the precentorship.

PREBENDARIES OF LLANFAIR, FIRST COMPORTION

M. John Crayford 1535.
    Occ. 1535 (*Valor* IV 436).

PREBENDARIES OF LLANFAIR, SECOND COMPORTION

    Hugh de Leversegge 1390.
    Estate ratif. 15 Oct. 1390 (*CPR. 1388–1392* p. 319).

    Hugh Holbache 1390, 1391.
    Estate ratif. 26 Nov. 1390 (*CPR. 1388–1392* p. 328). Royal gr. 8 Dec. 1391 (*CPR. 1391–1396* p. 4).

    John Repynton 1398–?
    Royal gr. 28 July 1398 (*CPR. 1396–1399* p. 404).

    John Honne 1437.
    Occ. 5 Oct. 1437 (*CPL.* VIII 656).

M. Robert Puleston ?–1517.
    D. as preb. before 15 Aug. 1517 (Nat. Libr. Wales, SA/MB/14 f. 18).

M. Hugh Puleston B.C.L. 1517–?
    Coll. 15 Aug. 1517 (Nat. Libr. Wales, SA/MB/14 f. 18). Occ. 1535 (*Valor* IV 436). Occ., not called preb., 3 Nov. 1547 (Nat. Libr. Wales, SA/MB/14 f. 18b). Occ. as preb. 1559/60 (*Thomas* I 290)—in a return of bp. Richard Davies (1559–1561).

---

[1] Dafydd Llwyd was possibly archdcn. 1461 as he was presented to the ch. of Dyserth 10 Aug. (*CPR. 1461–1467* p. 27; see p. 43 n. 2) but it is not clear whether he was presented as rector or vicar.

PREBENDARIES OF LLANNEFYDD

The prebend of Llannefydd was attached to the chancellorship.

PREBENDARIES OF MEIFOD

M. Lewis de Charlton Lic.Th. 1360, 1361.

Occ. as preb. of St Asaph and rector of Meifod[1] 30 March 1360 (*CPP*. 1 353). Occ. as preb. of Meifod 30 Jan. 1361 (*ibid*. p. 365). Bp. of Hereford in Sept.

M. William de Cherelton B.C.L. 1366.

Occ. as rector of Meifod[1] 19 Nov. 1366 (*Reg. Langham* p. 43).

M. John Trefnant D.C.L. ?–1389.

Vac. unnamed preb. in St Asaph and rectory of Meifod[1] 5 May 1389 when bp. of Hereford (*Reg. Trefnant* p. 1; *CPL*. IV 427).

Huw Bochenhull 1389–?
William Pregeet *or* **Excestre** 1389–?

Royal gr. to Bochenhull of preb. of Meifod 20 May (*CPR. 1388–1392* p. 38). Royal gr. to Pregeet 20 Dec. of preb. vac. by John Trefnant (*ibid*. p. 96). Second gr. of preb. of Meifod to Bochenhull 23 Feb. 1390 (*ibid*. p. 190).[2]

M. John Trefor D.Cn. & C.L. ?–1394.
Reginald de Hulton 1391.
John Mere ?–1392.

Trefor occ. as unnamed preb. 9 Nov. 1390 (*CPL*. IV 343). Litigation between Trefor and Hulton about the rectory of Meifod[1] mentioned 17 Nov. 1391, suit then undecided between two claimants (*ibid*. p. 427). Trefor exch. precentorship of Wells and preb. of Combe Undecima, Wells, with John Mere for rectory of Meifod, 18 July 1392 (*CPR. 1391–1396* p. 122). Vac. unnamed preb. in St Asaph when el. bp. 1394 (*ibid*. p. 580). Succeeded by Richard Prentys (see below).

Richard Prentys 1395–?

Royal gr. 10 June and 16 July 1395 of preb. vac. by John Trefor (*CPR. 1391–1396* pp. 580, 609; see above).

John Dyne ?–1397.

Exch. this preb. with Thomas Langley for ch. of St Alphege within Cripplegate, London, 15 Feb. 1397 (Lond., Guildhall, Reg. Braybroke f. 150).

Thomas Langley 1397–1406.

By exch. Feb. 1397. Estate ratif. 3 Apr. 1399 (*CPR. 1396–1399* p. 380)[3] and 24 May 1400 (*CPR. 1399–1401* p. 278). Bp. of Durham 1406.

William Tyrell 1406–1413.

Mand. adm. 28 Sept. 1406 (Lamb., Reg. Arundell 1 f. 310). Treasurer and preb. of Meliden 1413.

---

[1] The revenue of the ch. of Meifod, Montgom., provided the endowment of the preb. of Meifod. It therefore seems probable that the rectors of this ch. held the preb. of Meifod in St Asaph cath.

[2] This second gr. of the preb. to Bochenhull suggests that he was probably having difficulty in obtaining possession because of a rival claimant—Pregeet.

[3] The estate of John Carp as preb. of Llannefydd and 'parson' of Meifod was ratif. 28 Oct. 1399 (*CPR. 1399–1401* p. 25). He was probably vicar of Meifod, Langley's deputy and not a rival claimant for preb. of Meifod.

M. Owain Pole D.Cn.L. 1485–?
Royal gr. 30 Sept. 1485 of rectory of Meifod[1] (*CPR. 1485–1494* p. 10).

M. William Villiers D.C.L. ?–1494.
Exch. this preb. with Thomas Vele for ch. of Kirtling, Cambs., 7/15 March 1494 (*CPR. 1494–1509* p. 13; Norwich, Reg. Goldwell f. 184).

Thomas Vele 1494–?
By exch. March 1494. Mand. adm. 18 March (Norwich, Reg. Goldwell f. 184).

M. Dafydd Owain D.Th. ?–1558.
Occ. 1535 (*Valor* IV 436). D. before 24 May 1558 (Nat. Libr. Wales, SA/BR/1 f. 63).

PREBENDARIES OF MELIDEN

The prebend of Meliden was attached to the treasurership.

UNIDENTIFIED PREBENDARIES

William de Bricchull 1292, 1308.
Occ. 27 Jan. 1292 (*CPL.* I 548–9). Occ. 3 Aug. 1308 (*ibid.* II 42).

Richard Hering ?–1351.
D. as preb. before 4 May 1351 (*CPL.* III 364). Succeeded by Richard de Middleton (see below).

Richard de Middleton 1351–?
Prov. 4 May 1351 to preb. vac. by Richard Hering (*CPL.* III 364; see above). Did not obtain possession (*CPL.* III 567). Succeeded by John Harald (see below).

William de Courtenay 1355–?
Prov. 8 Feb. 1355 to canonry and preb. at St Asaph or Salisbury (*CPP.* I 284).

M. John Harald 1355–1361.
Prov. 8 Feb. 1355 to preb. vac. by Richard Hering (*CPL.* III 567; see above). Res. before 21 Jan. 1361 (*CPP.* I 362). Succeeded by John Gruffudd Ddu (see below).

M. John Gruffudd Ddu Sch.Cn.L. 1361–1366.
Prov. 21 Jan. 1361 to preb. vac. by John Harald (*CPP.* I 362; see above). D. before 14 Apr. 1366 without obtaining possession (*CPP.* I 525). Succeeded by Simon Latchebury (see below p. 47).

Nicholas de Louth 1361–1365.
Prov. 22 Jan. 1361 to canonry with reservn. of preb. (*CPP.* I 363). Exch. preb. with William de Langborough for preb. of Horton, Salisbury, 9 June 1365 (Salis., Reg. Wyville II ii ff. 309b, 311; see below).

M. William de Langborough 1365–?
By exch. with Nicholas de Louth for preb. of Horton, Salisbury, 9 June 1365 (Salis., Reg. Wyville II ii ff. 309b, 311; see above).

[1] See p. 45 n. 1.

Simon Latchebury 1366–1368.
Prov. 14 Apr. 1366 to preb. vac. by John Gruffudd Ddu (*CPP.* I 525; see above p. 46). Vac. preb. before 7 Jan. 1368 (*CPL.* IV 73). Succeeded by John Rhys (see below).

M. John Rhys Sch.C.L. ?–1368.
Mand. 7 Jan. 1368 to resign preb. (*CPL.* IV 73).

M. John Rhys Sch.C.L. 1368–?
Mand. to bp. of Bangor 7 Jan. 1368 to gr. Rhys preb. vac. by Simon Latchebury (*CPL.* IV 73; see above).

M. Ithel ap Bleddyn ap Madog ?–1382.
D. as preb. before 15 June 1382 (*CPR. 1381–1385* p. 130). Succeeded by Richard Clifford (see below).

Richard Clifford 1382–?
Royal gr. 15 June 1382 of preb. vac. by Ithel ap Bleddyn ap Madog (*CPR. 1381–1385* p. 130; see above). ? Held preb. until 1400 when el. bp. of Bath and Wells.

David Brackerne ?–1390.
Vac. preb. before 27 May 1390 (*CPR. 1388–1392* p. 256). Succeeded by Nicholas ap Philip (see below).

Nicholas ap Philip 1390.
Estate ratif. 27 May 1390 in preb. vac. by David Brackerne (*CPR. 1388–1392* p. 256; see above).

Hywel Trefnant *or* ap Dafydd ?–1391.
D. as preb. before 1 Dec. 1391 (*CPR. 1391–1396* p. 3). Succeeded by John Prata (see below).

John Prata 1391–?
Prov. n.d., gr. royal lic. 1 Dec. 1391 to execute prov. to preb. vac. by Hywel Trefnant (*CPR. 1391–1396* p. 3; see above).

M. Matthew de Hanemere D.C.L. ?–1398.
Vac. preb. before 5 March 1398 (*CPR. 1396–1399* p. 258). Succeeded by Edward Trefor (see below).

M. Edward Trefor 1398.
Estate ratif. 5 March 1398 in preb. vac. by Matthew de Hanemere (*CPR. 1396–1399* p. 258; see above).

M. Lewis Aber ?–1398.
Held preb. 21 Aug. 1398 when el. bp. of Bangor (*CPL.* v 99). Succeeded by David Gele (see below).

Dafydd Gele 1398–?
Prov. 21 Aug. 1398 to preb. vac. by Lewis Aber (*CPL.* v 99; see above).

M. Adam de Usk D.C.L. 1404.
Occ. 11 Nov. 1404 (*CPL.* VI 44–5).

Thomas Harlyng 1415.
Occ. 10 March 1415 (*CPL.* VI 496).

Ralph Wellys 1427.
Occ. 14 Dec. 1427 (*CPL.* VIII 19–20).

Thomas Banastre 1431.
Occ. 22 Sept. 1431 (*CPL.* VIII 462).

M. **Andrew Holes** Lic.Cn.L. 1433, 1440.
Occ. 29 Aug. 1433 (*CPL.* VIII 459–60). Occ. 24 Feb. 1440 (*ibid.* IX 81–2).

Richard Forest 1435.
Occ. 31 Aug. 1435 (*CPL.* VIII 527).

M. **John Sutton** M.A. 1447.
Occ. 17 Oct. 1447 (*CPL.* X 8).

John Clerk ?–1458.
Vac. preb. before 26 Oct. 1458 (*CPR. 1452–1461* p. 462). Succeeded by Gilbert Haydok (see below).

M. **Gilbert Haydok** D.Th. 1458–?
Royal gr. 26 Oct. 1458 of preb. vac. by John Clerk (*CPR. 1452–1461* p. 462; see above). ? Held preb. until d., 17 July/29 Nov. 1481 (PCC 13 Logge).

M. **Thomas Eggecombe** B.Cn. & C.L. ?–1467.
Res. preb. before 15 May 1467 (*Reg. Bourgchier* p. 289). Succeeded by Robert Slimbridge (see below).

M. **Robert Slimbridge** B.Cn. & C.L. 1467–?
Coll. by abp. 15 May 1467 to preb. vac. by Thomas Eggecombe (*Reg. Bourgchier* p. 289; see above). ? Held preb. until d., 5 Dec. 1504/24 Nov. 1505 (PCC 41 Holgrave).

Richard Lyde 1513.
Occ. 11 Feb. 1513 (PCC 23 Fetiplace).

Robert ap Rhys 1513, 1518.
Occ. as preb. 11 Feb. 1513 (PCC 23 Fetiplace). Occ. as can. 12 July 1518 (Lamb., Reg. Warham I f. 21b).

Adam Bekensall 1535.
Occ. 1535 (*Valor* IV 436).

Ralph Brikenhead 1535, 1536.
Occ. 1535 (*Valor* IV 436). Occ. 7 June 1536 (Lamb., Reg. Cranmer f. 195b).

M. **Arthur Bulkeley** D.Cn.L. 1535, 1541.
Occ. 1535 (*Valor* IV 436). Occ. 22 Oct. 1541, then gr. royal lic. to hold preb. *in commendam* with bpc. of Bangor (*L. & P.* XVI No. 1391 (6)).

Dafydd ap Hywel 1535.
Occ. 1535 (*Valor* IV 436).

John Gruffudd 1535.
Occ. 1535 (*Valor* IV 436).

Richard Harrison 1535.
Occ. 1535 (*Valor* IV 436).

M. **Geoffrey Ruthyn** B.C.L. 1535, 1536.
Occ. 1535 (*Valor* IV 436). Occ. 7 June 1536 (Lamb., Reg. Cranmer f. 195b).

CANONS WITH EXPECTATION OF PREBENDS

M. Griffin de Treisnorit 1317–?
Prov. 14 May 1317 (*CPL.* II 155). Occ. as can. 18 Sept. 1324 (*ibid.* p. 241).

M. John Trefor B.Th. 1343–1346.
Prov. 29 Jan. 1343 (*CPL.* III 100). Bp. of St Asaph 1346.

M. John Toppan D.C.L. 1343–?
Prov. 20 Nov. 1343 (*CPL.* III 134). Occ. as can. 11 Apr. 1347 (*ibid.* p. 238).

John de Hamslape 1344–?
Prov. 22 Oct. 1344 (*CPL.* III 101).

M. Ithel ap Robert B.C.L. 1357–?
Prov. 17 Aug. 1357 (*CPP.* I 300–1).

M. John Landreyn Sch.Th., B.M. 1363–?
Prov. 14 Feb. 1363 (*CPP.* I 403).

M. Henry Witherton B.C.L. 1363–1366.
Prov. 1363 (*CPP.* I 436). Petitioned 24 March 1366 to be permitted to resign because ignorant of the language in those parts (*ibid.* p. 519).

CANONS OF ST ASAPH

Elias 1306.
Occ. 1306 (Nat. Libr. Wales, Add. MS. 7011 D p. 18).

Madog Goch 1307.
Occ. 1307 (*Rot. Parl.* I 190).

M. Dafydd ap Bleddyn 1314.
Occ. 25 Jan. and 18 July 1314 (P.R.O., C 84/18/9; *CPR. 1313–1317* p. 160). El. bp. of St Asaph July/Sept.

Madog ab Isaac 1314.
Occ. 25 Jan. 1314 (P.R.O., C 84/18/9).

Cynwrig ap Ros 1328.
Occ. 4 and 22 Apr. 1328 (Cant., Reg. Q ff. 170–170b).

M. Griffin Trefor D.Cn.L. 1343, 1346.
Occ. 4 July 1343 (*CPL.* III 130). Occ. 1 Aug. 1346 (*ibid.* p. 224).

M. Matthew Trefor D.C.L. 1343, 1346.
Occ. 20 Nov. 1343 (*CPL.* III 100). Occ. 2 July 1346 (*ibid.* p. 221).

Einion ab Iorwerth 1343, 1345.
Occ. 20 Nov. 1343 (*CPL.* III 100). Occ. 24 Nov. 1345 (*Cal. Anct. Correspondence* p. 240).

M. Robert de Pinchbeck 1344–?
Prov. 6 Aug. 1344 (*CPL.* III 150).

Richard de Oswestry 1345.
Occ. Oct./Nov. 1345 (*Cal. Anct. Correspondence* p. 240).

Hywel Cyffin *junior* 1379, 1393.
Occ. 11 Apr. 1379 (Lincoln, Reg. x (Buckingham) f. 229b). Occ. 3 Oct. 1393 (P.R.O., C 84/36/10).

Walter Brandoun 1387.
Occ. 20 July 1387 (*CPR. 1385–1389* p. 434).

Lewis Trefor 1393.
Occ. 3 Oct. 1393 (P.R.O., C 84/36/10).

M. **John Blodwel** B.C.L. 1420, 1422.
Occ. 24 May 1420 (*Reg. Chichele* I 66). Occ. 12 Oct. 1422 (*CPL.* VII 211–12).

Hywel Griffin 1424.
Occ. 29 May 1424 (*Reg. T. Spofford*, ed. A. T. Bannister (Canterbury and York Soc., xxiii) p. 76).

Thomas Pellichon 1427.
William Spechell 1427.
Nicholas Clerc *or* **Smyth** 1427.
Pellichon occ. 6 Nov. 1427 (*CPL.* VII 496). Had then obtained favourable verdict in suit between himself and Spechell about canonry, but while suit still pending Clerc had intruded himself and still in possession of canonry (*ibid.*).

M. **Benedict Combe** 1429.
Occ. 5 Oct. 1429 (*Reg. Chichele* I 258).

M. **John Lassy** 1463.
Occ. 6 Nov. 1463 (*CPL.* XI 651–2).

Robert Madog 1518.
Occ. 12 July 1518 (Lamb., Reg. Warham I f. 21b).

St Davids 1300-1541

MANUSCRIPT MATERIAL

National Library of Wales, *Aberystwyth*

SD Ch. B/1.	St Davids chapter account book.
SD/BR/2.	Bishops' registers 1554–1565.

British Museum

Harley MS. 1249.	Register of St Davids—sixteenth-century transcript.
Harley MS. 6280.	Liber Statutorum of St Davids—sixteenth-century transcript.

Canterbury Cathedral Library

Registers A, Q, S, T.

Lambeth Palace Library

The registers of the archbishops of Canterbury from Reynolds to Cranmer, 1314–1555.

Somerset House

PCC: Registers of wills proved in the prerogative court of Canterbury.

Additional registers of the bishops of St Davids were available when Edward Yardley, archdeacon of Cardigan 1739–1770, compiled *Menevia Sacra*. He used the registers of bp. Benedict Nicholls, 1417–1433, and Thomas Rodburn, 1433–1442 which are now completely lost, and additional parts of the register of Henry Chichele, 1407–1414 and of John Hiot his vicar general, of which now only fragments survive. These four registers have here been used from *Menevia Sacra* (Cambrian Archaeol. Assoc., 1927), with reference given to the folio numbers noted by archdeacon Yardley and the page in his printed work.

M. David Martin 1293–1328.

[**Thomas de Goldesburgh** 1293.]

Lic. el. gr. 18 May 1293 (*CPR. 1292–1301* p. 15). Martin el. n.d., royal assent sought 27 July (P.R.O., C 84/11/25). Royal assent gr. 28 July (*CPR. 1292–1301* p. 35). Goldesburgh had been el. by minority of chapt.—proctor arrived at Canterbury 18 Sept., case heard 30 Sept., when decided that Martin rightful bp. because had received fourteen votes out of twenty, and Goldesburgh had only six votes (Cant., Reg. Q ff. 51/66–51b/66b). El. of Martin conf. by prior of Canterbury 1 Oct. (P.R.O., C 84/11/31). Mand. 11 Oct. to restore temps. to Martin (*CPR. 1292–1301* p. 39). Martin gr. safe conduct 9 Nov. to go to curia because Goldesburgh still claiming bpc. (*ibid.* p. 40). Litigation at curia, k. sent letter 16 Aug. 1295 commending Martin (*CCR. 1288–1296* p. 451). Martin prov. 1296 (*CPL.* I 564). Cons. 30 Sept. at Rome by card. bp. of Ostia (Cant., Reg. A f. 303b/248b). Mand. to restore temps. 24 Jan. 1297 (*CPR. 1292–1301* p. 230). D. 9 March 1328 (Cant., Reg. Q f. 161b).

M. Henry de Gower D.Cn. & C.L. 1328–1347.

Lic. el sought 17 March 1328 (P.R.O., C 84/22/4). Lic. el. gr. 26 March (*CPR. 1327–1330* p. 253). El. 21 Apr. (Cant., Reg. Q f. 162). Royal assent 1 May (*CPR. 1327–1330* p. 259). Conf. by prior of Canterbury 21 May (P.R.O., C 84/22/9). Temps. 26 May (*CPR. 1327–1330* p. 273). Cons. 12 June at Canterbury (Cant., Reg. A f. 304/249). D. before 4 May 1347 (P.R.O., C 84/25/21).

[**M. William de Carrewe** 1347.]

M. John de Thoresby B.C.L. 1347–1349.

Lic. el. sought 4 May 1347 (P.R.O., C 84/25/12). Lic. el. gr. 15 May (*CPR. 1345–1348* pp. 292–3). Royal assent to el. of Carrewe 30 June (*ibid.* p. 344). El. set aside because Thoresby had been prov. 23 May (*CPL.* III 240). Temps. 14 July (*CPR. 1345–1348* p. 361). Cons. 23 Sept. at Otford, Kent (*R.S.A.*). Trans. to Worcester 1349.

M. Reginald Brian Lic.C.L. 1349–1352.

Prov. 11 Sept. 1349 (Lamb., Reg. Islip f. 9b). Lic. *alibi cons.* 18 Oct. (*CPP.* I 181). Temps. 15 Jan. 1350 (*CPR. 1348–1350* p. 445). Spir. 18 Jan. (Lamb., Reg. Islip ff. 9b–10). Cons. 23 Sept. (*ibid.* f. 31). Trans. to Worcester 1352.

M. Thomas Fastolf D.C.L. 1352–1361.

Prov. 22 Oct. 1352 (Lamb., Reg. Islip ff. 63b–64). Cons. n.d. at Rome by card. bp. of Tusculum (Cant., Reg. A f. 304/249). Spir. 29 March 1353 (Lamb., Reg. Islip f. 66b). Temps. 4 June (*CPR. 1350–1354* p. 462). Profession 15 March 1358 (Cant., Reg. A f. 304/249).[1] D. 19 June/1 July 1361 (Lamb., Reg. Islip f. 233).

M. Adam de Houghton D.C.L. 1361–1389.

Prov. 20 Sept. 1361 (Lamb., Reg. Islip ff. 233–233b). Spir. 15 Nov. (*ibid.* f. 233b). Temps. 8 Dec. (*CPR. 1361–1364* p. 122). Cons. 2 Jan. 1362 (*R.S.A.*). D. before 10 Feb. 1389 (P.R.O., C 84/34/29).

[1] Fastolf made his profession before the high altar at Canterbury 'Absentibus dominis archiepiscopo et priore'.

M. John Gilbert[1] O.P., D.Th. 1389–1397.

Lic. el. sought 10 Feb. 1389 (P.R.O., C 84/34/29). Lic. el. gr. 27 Feb. (*CPR. 1388–1392* p. 14). Trans. from Hereford 5 May (Lamb., Reg. Courtenay ff. 323b–324). Temps. 12 July (*CPR. 1388–1392* p. 89). Profession to abp. s.d. (Lamb., Reg. Courtenay f. 324). D. 28 July 1397 (Lamb., Reg. Arundell 1 f. 458).

Guy de Mona 1397–1407.

Lic. el. gr. 16 Aug. 1397 (*CPR. 1396–1399* p. 186). Prov. 30 Aug. (*CPL.* v 22). Lic. *alibi cons.* 1 Sept. (*ibid.* p. 72). Mand. to deliver spir. 27 Oct. (Lamb., Reg. Arundell 1 f. 458). Cons. 11 Nov. at Abingdon, Berks. (*Reg. St Davids* 1 3). Profession to abp. 9 Oct. 1401 (Lamb., Reg. Arundell 1 f. 13). D. 31 Aug. 1407 (*Menevia Sacra* p. 60).

M. Henry Chichele D.C.L. 1407–1414.

Lic. el. gr. 2 Oct. 1407 (*CPR. 1405–1408* p. 364). Prov. 4 Oct.[2] (Lamb., Reg. Arundell 1 ff. 42–42b). Cons. March 1408 at Siena (*Reg. Chichele* 1 p. xxviii). Temps. 3 Apr. (*CPR. 1405–1408* p. 426). Spir. 26 Aug. (Lamb., Reg. Arundell 1 f. 43). Profession to abp. s.d. (*ibid.*). Enthroned 20 May 1411 (Reg. Chichele—in *Menevia Sacra* p. 62). Abp. of Canterbury 1414.

M. John Catryk Lic.Cn.L. 1414–1415.

Prov. 27 Apr. 1414 (*CPL.* vi 454). Cons. by pope n.d. (*Reg. Chichele* 1 15). Temps. 2 June (*CPR. 1413–1416* p. 198). Spir. 18 July (*Reg. Chichele* 1 15). Profession to abp. s.d. (*ibid.* pp. 14–15). Trans. to Coventry and Lichfield 1415.

M. Stephen Patryngton O.Carm., D.Th. 1415–1417.

Prov. 1 Feb. 1415 (*CPL.* vi 350). Lic. *alibi cons.* 3 Feb. (*ibid.* p. 458). Temps. 16 June (*CPR. 1413–1416* p. 336). Cons. at Maidstone, Kent, 19 June (*Reg. Chichele* 1 24–5). Trans. to Chichester 1417.

M. Benedict Nicholls B.Cn.L. 1417–1433.

Trans. from Bangor 15 Dec. 1417 (*Reg. Chichele* 1 40–1). Mand. to abp. 21 Dec. to receive profession (*ibid.* p. 41). Profession to abp. 12 Feb. 1418 (*ibid.* p. 42). Temps. 1 June (*CPR. 1416–1422* pp. 151–2). Profession to chapt. at St Davids 16 Oct. (Brit. Mus., Harley MS. 6280 ff. 101b–102). D. 14 June/16 July 1433 (*Reg. Chichele* II 484–5; *CPR. 1429–1436* p. 282).

M. Thomas Rodburn Lic.Th. 1433–1442.

Lic. el. gr. 16 July 1433 (*CPR. 1429–1436* p.292). Prov. 5 Oct. (*Reg. Chichele* 1 118). Lic. *alibi cons.* 19 Oct. (Cant., Reg. S f. 126/116). Temps. 16 Dec. (*CPR. 1429–1436* p. 328). Cons. 31 Jan. 1434 (*R.S.A.*). D. before 27 June 1442 (*CPL.* ix 297).

M. William Lyndwood D.Cn. & C.L. 1442–1446.

Prov. 27 June 1442 (*CPL.* ix 297). Lic. *alibi cons.* 30 June (*ibid.* p. 253). Lic. el. gr. 3 July (*CPR. 1441–1446* p. 102). Temps. 14 Aug. (*ibid.* p. 91). Cons. 26 Aug./2 Oct. (*R.S.A.*; Lamb., Reg. Stafford f. 142). D. 21 Oct. 1446 (Brit. Mus., Cotton MS. Faustina B. viii ff. 6b, 52).

M. John Langton Lic.Cn.L. 1447.

Lic. el. sought 8 Nov. 1446 (P.R.O., C 84/46/41). Prov. 23 Jan. 1447 (Lamb.,

---

[1] Richard de Medford is said to have been nominated by the king as bp. of St Davids 1389 (*Menevia Sacra* p. 58), but no evidence has been found for this. He had been prov. to the bpc. of Chichester 17 Nov. 1388 and made profession to abp. 7 May 1389 (Lamb., Reg. Courtenay f. 325).

[2] Griffin le Yonge obtained an abortive prov. to St Davids in 1407 by the schismatic pope Benedict XIII (*Williams* p. 224).

Reg. Stafford ff. 25–25b). Lic. *alibi cons.* 26 Jan. (*CPL.* IX 562). Lic. el. gr. 25 Feb. (*CPR. 1446–1452* p. 34). Temps. 2 March (*ibid.* p. 50). Profession to abp. 19 March (Lamb., Reg. Stafford f. 25b). Commission by abp. for cons. 29 Apr. (*ibid.* f. 26). Cons. 7 May in King's College, Cambridge (*R.S.A.*). D. 22 May (*Emden, Reg. Camb.* p. 352).

M. **John de la Bere** B.Cn.L. 1447–1460.

Prov. 15 Sept. 1447 (*CPL.* X 295). Cons. n.d. by abp.[1] (Lamb., Reg. Stafford f. 28). Profession to abp. 13 Nov. (*ibid.*). Temps. 14 Nov. (*CPR. 1446–1452* p. 114). Res. bpc. 23 July 1460 (*CPL.* XI 410–11). Gr. royal pardon 5 Feb. 1461 but not restored to bpc. (*Foedera* V i 103).

M. **Robert Tully** O.S.B., D.Th. 1460–1482.

Prov. 23 July 1460 (*CPL.* XI 410–11). Lic. *alibi cons.* 28 Aug. (Cant., Reg. S ff. 205b–206). Temps. 20 Oct. (*CPR. 1452–1461* p. 635). D. before 26 Feb. 1482 (*CPR. 1476–1485* p. 259).

M. **Richard Martin** D.Cn.L. 1482–1483.

Custody of temps. gr. 26 Feb. 1482 (*CPR. 1476–1485* p. 259). Prov. 26 Apr. (*CPL.* XIII ii 743). Lic. *alibi cons.* 27 Apr. and 10 June (*ibid.* pp. 743–4; Cant., Reg. S f. 324b). Temps. 1 July (*CPR. 1476–1485* p. 307). Profession to abp. 8 July (*Reg. Bourgchier* p. 48). Cons. 28 July (*Reg. St Davids* II 449). D. 25 March[2] 1483 (Cambridge, Trinity College MS. 224 f. 1).

M. **Thomas Langton** D.Th., D.Cn.L. 1483–1485.

Custody of temps. gr. 21 May 1483 (*CPR. 1476–1485* p. 348) and 6 July (*ibid.* p. 361). Prov. 4 July (*CPL.* XIII ii 826). Lic. *alibi cons.* 23 Aug. (Cant., Reg. S ff. 328–328b). Profession to abp. 3 Sept. (*Reg. Bourgchier* p. 59). Cons. c. 7 Sept. (*R.S.A.*). Temps. 25 March 1484 (*Foedera* V iv 145). Trans. to Salisbury 1485.

M. **Huw Pavy** B.C.L. 1485–1496.

Custody of temps. gr. 2 May 1485 (*CPR. 1476–1485* p. 527). Prov. 6 May (*Eubel* II 209). Lic. *alibi cons.* 22 Sept. (Cant., Reg. S f. 341). Cons. 9 Oct. by bps. of Bath and Wells and Cloyne, Ireland (*Reg. St Davids* II 459). Plenary restitution of temps. 19 Sept. 1486 (*CPR. 1485–1494* p. 130). D. 3 May/3 Aug. 1496 (PCC 28 Horne; *Eubel* II 209).

M. **John Morgan** *or* **Young** B.Cn.L. 1496–1504.

Prov. 3 Aug. 1496 (*Eubel* II 209). Custody of temps. gr. 3 Nov. (*CPR. 1494–1509* p. 76). Lic. *alibi cons.* 12 Nov. (Cant., Reg. S f. 409). Temps. 23 Nov. (*CPR. 1494–1509* p. 78). D. 24 Apr./19 May 1504 (PCC 8 Holgrave).

M. **Robert Sherbourne** B.M. 1505–1508.

Prov. 5 Jan. 1505 (*Eubel* III 259). Temps. 12 Apr. (*CPR. 1494–1509* p. 414). Lic. *alibi cons.* 24 Apr. (Lamb., Reg. Warham I f. 11b). Cons. 11 May (*R.S.A.*). Trans. to Chichester 1508.

M. **Edward Fychan** D.Cn.L. 1509–1523.

Prov. 13 June 1509 (Lamb., Reg. Warham I ff. 12b–13). Nominated by k. 15 July (*L. & P.* I i No. 393). Lic. *alibi cons.* 20 July (Lamb., Reg. Warham I f. 13). Cons. by

---

[1] In his profession to the abp. on 13 Nov. 1447, de la Bere stated 'A vobis consecrandus', which suggests that his consecration had not yet taken place.

[2] Richard Martin's obit was observed at Canterbury on 19 Nov. (Brit. Mus., Arundel MS. 68 f. 48b). It is probable that the March date is correct since Langton, his successor, was gr. custody of the temps. of the bpc. in May.

abp. at Lambeth 22 July (*ibid.*). Profession to abp. s.d. (*ibid.*). Temps. 2 Aug. (*L. & P.* 1 i No. 158 (13)). D. before 27 Jan. 1523 (PCC 2 Bodfelde).

M. Richard Rawlings D.Th. 1523–1536.

Prov. 11 March 1523 (Lamb., Reg. Warham I f. 24b). Lic. *alibi cons.* 22 Apr. (Cant., Reg. T f. 214b). Temps. 24 Apr. (*Foedera* VI i 212). Cons. by abp. at Lambeth 26 Apr. (Lamb., Reg. Warham I f. 25). D. 18 Feb. 1536 (Lamb., Reg. Cranmer ff. 205b–206).

M. William Barlow O.Can.S.A., D.Th. 1536–1548.

El. 10 Apr. 1536 after being recommended to chapt. by k. (Lamb., Reg. Cranmer f. 206). Royal assent 20 Apr. (*ibid.* ff. 205–205b). Conf. by abp. 21 Apr. (*ibid.* f. 205). Trans. to Bath and Wells 1548.

PRECENTORS OF ST DAVIDS

Note: The prebend of Lampeter-pont-Stephen was attached to the precentorship.

Thomas Barry 1300.

Thomas occ. 1296 (*CPL.* 1 564). Thomas Barry occ. 14 June 1300 (*Reg. Corbridge* I 202).

M. Richard de Mosslewyke 1328.

Occ. 17 March and 21 May 1328 (P.R.O., C 84/22/4; Cant., Reg. Q f. 166).

M. David Barret 1335.

Occ. 14 Feb. 1335 (Brit. Mus., Harley MS. 6280 f. 58b).

M. Adam de Houghton 1339.

Occ. 26 July 1339 (Brit. Mus., Harley MS. 6280 f. 57b).

David Lee 1350–?[1]

Royal gr. 6 Feb. 1350 (*CPR. 1348–1350* p. 461). Occ. 19 June 1361 (Lamb., Reg. Islip f. 233).

M. Henry Rhydderch 1383.

Occ. 8 June 1383 (*Reg. St Davids* II 629).

John Nook ?–1413.
M. John Hiot 1397.

Estate of Nook ratif. 20 June 1393 (*CPR. 1391–1396* p. 56). Hiot occ. as preb. of Lampeter-pont-Stephen 15 Oct. 1397 (*CPR. 1396–1399* p. 219). Nook regained possession, since d. as precentor before 8 Aug. 1413 (Reg. Chichele f. 12b—in *Menevia Sacra* p. 128).

Thomas Wollaston 1413–1437.

Coll. 8 Aug. 1413 (Reg. Chichele f. 12b—*in Menevia Sacra* p. 128). D. before 29 Sept. 1437 (Reg. Rodburn ff. 104, 111b— in *Menevia Sacra* p. 129).

Huw ab Owain 1437–1486.

Coll. 29 Sept. 1437 (Reg. Rodburn ff. 104, 111b—in *Menevia Sacra* p. 129). D. before 28 July 1486 (*Reg. St Davids* II 469).

---

[1] There is no evidence that David Barret was precentor 1354 as stated by Le Neve-Hardy.

M. **Richard Machyn** B.Cn.L. 1486–1492.
Coll. 28 July 1486 (*Reg. St Davids* II 469). D. before 28 Nov. 1492 (*ibid.* p. 641).

M. **John Hywel**[1] B.Cn.L. 1492–?
Coll. 28 Nov. 1492 (*Reg. St Davids* II 641). Occ. 8 July 1504 (Lamb., Reg. Warham II f. 223).

Lewis ap Rhys 1509.
Occ. 15 Oct. 1509 (PCC 23 Bennett).

M. **Thomas Llwyd**[2] B.C.L. ?–1546/7.
Occ. 1529 (*L. & P.* IV iii No. 6047 p. 2701). D. 21 Dec. 1546/14 Dec. 1547 (PCC 51 Alen).

CHANCELLORS OF ST DAVIDS

Note : The prebend of Llawhaden was attached to the chancellorship.

David Franceys 1326, 1328.
Occ. 1326 (*Black Book of St David's*, ed. J. W. Willis-Bund (Cymmrodorion Record Soc., 1902) p. 31). Occ. 21 May 1328 (Cant., Reg. Q f. 166).

John Gome 1333.
Occ. 3 Feb. 1333 (Brit. Mus., Harley MS. 6280 f. 81).

M. **John Franceys** 1335.
Occ. 14 Feb. 1335 (Brit. Mus., Harley MS. 6280 f. 59).

M. **David Barret** 1339, 1348.
Occ. 26 July 1339 (Brit. Mus., Harley MS. 6280 f. 57b). Occ. 15 Sept. 1348 (*ibid.* f. 57).

William de Tilney 1360.
Occ. 10 May 1360 (*CPP.* I 354).

M. **John David** 1361–1407.
Royal gr. 19 Nov. 1361 (*CPR. 1361–1364* p. 114). D. before 21 Jan. 1407 (*Reg. St Davids* I 379).

M. **John Colle** Sch.C.L. 1407–1417.
Coll. 21 Jan. 1407 (*Reg. St Davids* I 379). Exch. chancellorship with Edmund Lacy for ch. of Marnhull, Dors., 16 Jan. 1417 (Salis., Reg. Hallum f. 52).

M. **Edmund Lacy** D.Th. 1417.
By exch. Jan. 1417. Bp. of Hereford, cons. 18 Apr.

M. **Dafydd ap Rhys** Lic.C.L. ?–1426.
Occ. c. 20 March 1418 (Bodl. Libr., MS. Arch. Selden B. 23 f. 93b). Exch. chancellorship with Richard Wogan for a cursal preb. 28 March 1426 (Reg. Nicholls f. 47b—in *Menevia Sacra* p. 144).

[1] William Walter had been prov. to the 'deanery' of St Davids c. 1492 and had been imprisoned by the bp. in Llawhaden castle for accepting this prov. (*Reg. St Davids* II 681–3). Papal mand. 22 Oct. 1493 that Walter should be released (*ibid.*). It is probable that Walter had been prov. to the precentorship which was vac. 1492 since the precentor was head of the St Davids chapt. and there was no dn. of St Davids until the office was created in the nineteenth century (*Williams* pp. 315–16, 315 n. 2).

[2] Thomas Llwyd occ. as chancellor 19 June 1539 (PCC 36 Alenger). This must have been a scribal error for precentor or 'chantor' since he appears to have held that office until his d., 1546/7.

Richard Wogan 1426–?

By exch. March 1426. Occ. 17 June 1437 (Reg. Rodburn f. 126b—in *Menevia Sacra* p. 144).

M. Richard Caunton D.Cn. & C.L. 1453.

Occ. 19 Apr. 1453 (*CPL.* x 132–3).[1]

John ap Hywel ?–1487.

D. as chancellor before 29 Dec. 1487 (*Reg. St Davids* II 513).

M. Lewis ap John B.Cn. & C.L. 1487–1490.

Coll. 29 Dec. 1487 (*Reg. St Davids* II 513). D. before 25 Jan. 1490 (*ibid.* p. 581).

John Denby 1490–1492.

Coll. 25 Jan. 1490 (*Reg. St Davids* II 581). Archdcn. of St Davids 1492.

M. John Talley D.C.L. ?–1509.

Occ. 30 July 1493 (*Reg. St Davids* II 663). D. 15 Oct./15 Dec. 1509 (PCC 23 Bennett).

William Stradling ?–1539.

Occ. 2 March 1512 (PCC 30 Fetiplace). D. 8 June/31 Oct. 1539 (PCC 32 Dyngeley).[2]

TREASURERS OF ST DAVIDS

Note: The prebend of Llandyssilio-gogo was attached to the treasurership.

William de Orleyns 1328.

Occ. 17 March and 21 Apr. 1328 (P.R.O., C 84/22/4; Cant., Reg. Q f. 163).

M. David Barret 1333.

Occ. 1 March 1333 (Brit. Mus., Harley MS. 6280 f. 60).

John de Crickhowell 1335.

Occ. 14 Feb. 1335 (Brit. Mus., Harley MS. 6280 f. 58b).

Philip de Crickhowell 1339.

Occ. 26 July 1339 (Brit. Mus., Harley MS. 6280 f. 57b).

Walter de Trefdyn 1342, 1352.

Occ. 27 May 1342 (Brit. Mus., Harley MS. 6280 f. 15). Occ. 18 May 1352 (*ibid.* f. 35b).

Robert Rhys 1361–?

Royal gr. 5 Aug. 1361 (*CPR. 1361–1364* p. 48).

M. William Wroth D.C.L. ?–1365.

Exch. treasurership with Dafydd Fychan for free chaps. of Bockingfold, in Goudhurst, and Lydd, Kent, and preb. of Caron, Llanddewi Brefi colleg. ch., Card., 29 Jan. 1365 (Lamb., Reg. Islip f. 306).

Dafydd Fychan 1365–?

By exch. Jan. 1365. Occ. 12 Oct. 1366 (*Reg. Langham* p. 31).

---

[1] Caunton must have res. the chancellorship by 1459 when he occ. as archdcn. of St Davids. See p. 60.

[2] See p. 57 n. 2.

M. **Lewis Aber** 1383, 1389.
Occ. 8 June 1383 (*Reg. St Davids* II 629). Occ. 6 May 1389 (Lamb., Reg. Courtenay f. 167). ? Held treasurership until 1398 when el. bp. of Bangor.

M. **Roger Basset** Lic.C.L. 1398–1416.
  Maurice Rhiwlas 1404–?
Treasurership reserved for Basset 21 Aug. 1398 (*CPL.* V 179). Estate ratif. 31 Jan. 1399 (*CPR. 1396–1399* p. 451). Papal mand. to deprive him for plurality 15 May 1404 and adm. Rhiwlas if fit in Latin (*CPL.* IV 580). Basset retained possession since d. as treasurer, 16/26 Sept. 1416 (PCC 35 Marche).

  Roger de Bottal ?–1437.
Occ. 3 May 1421 (Reg. Nicholls f. 36—in *Menevia Sacra* p. 160). Exch. treasurership with John Schipton for a cursal preb. 4 March 1437 (Reg. Rodburn f. 106—in *Menevia Sacra* pp. 160, 288).

M. **John Schipton** 1437–?
By exch. March 1437. Occ. 21 Oct. 1446 (Lamb., Reg. Stafford f. 25).

M. **Owain Pole** B.Cn. & C.L. ?–1509.
Occ. 29 Jan. 1476 (*CPL.* XIII ii 493–4). D. 10/18 Dec. 1509 (PCC 26 Bennett; *Reg. R. Mayew*, ed. A. T. Bannister (Canterbury and York Soc., xxvii) p. 277).

M. **John Gruffudd** ?–1523.
D. as treasurer 3 Apr./2 May 1523 (PCC 8 Bodfelde).

  John Lewis ?–1541.
Occ. 18 July 1534 (*L. & P.* VII No. 1024 p. 393). D. before 2 Nov. 1541 (PCC 36 Alenger).

ARCHDEACONS OF ST DAVIDS

Note: The prebend of Mydrim was attached to this archdeaconry.

John 1296.
Occ. 1296, as John 'called Folk' (*CPL.* I 564). 'J' occ. 1307 (*Rot. Parl.* I 190).

M. **Henry de Gower**[1] D.Cn. & C.L. ?–1328.
Archdcn. 1328 when el. bp. of St Davids (*CPR. 1327–1330* p. 253).

  David Franceys 1333.
Occ. 3 Feb. 1333 (Brit. Mus., Harley MS. 6280 f. 81).

  Philip de Caunton 1335.
Occ. 14 Feb. 1335 (Brit. Mus., Harley MS. 6280 f. 58b).

  John Franceys 1342, 1345.
Occ. 27 May 1342 (Brit. Mus., Harley MS. 6280 f. 15). Occ. 9 Apr. 1345 (*ibid.* f. 42b).

  John Faukes ?–1349.
Occ. 17 Apr. 1347 (*CPL.* III 249). D. before 13 Oct. 1349 (*ibid.* p. 335).

M. **Richard Cleangre** D.Th. 1349–?
Papal conf. 13 Oct. 1349 of coll. to archdcnry by bp. (*CPL.* III 335).

---

[1] There is no evidence that Philip was archdcn. in 1319 as stated by Le Neve-Hardy.

John Goch 1349, 1359.

Occ. 8 Dec. 1349 (*CPL.* III 315). Occ. 6 Sept. 1359 (*CCR. 1354-1360* p. 643).

M. Adam de Bokelyn *or* **Robelyn** B.Cn.L. 1363-?

Royal gr. 17 Feb. 1363 (*CPR. 1361-1364* p. 302). Occ. 8 June 1383 (*Reg. St Davids* II 629).

John de Bowland ?-1400.

Occ. 22 May 1388 (*CCR. 1385-1389* p. 494). Preb. of Caerfai 1400.[1]

M. John Hiot 1400-1420.

Coll. 24 June 1400[1] (*Reg. St Davids* I 173-5). Estate ratif. 28 Feb. 1401 (*CPR. 1401-1405* p. 13). D. before 31 May 1420 (Reg. Nicholls f. 25b—in *Menevia Sacra* p. 177).

John Thomas 1420.

Coll. 31 May 1420 (Reg. Nicholls f. 25b—in *Menevia Sacra* p. 177). Exch. archdcnry with Edmund Nicholls for ch. of Kings Ripton, Hunts., 12 June/20 July (*CPR. 1416-1422* p. 280; Lincoln, Reg. XVI (Fleming) ff. 105-105b).

Edmund Nicholls 1420-1422.

By exch. June/July 1420. Certif. that exch. canonical 31 Aug. (Lincoln, Reg. XVI (Fleming) f. 105b). Exch. archdcnry and a preb. in Bangor with William Ryley for ch. of Hemingford Abbots, Hunts., 12/22/24 Nov. 1422 (*ibid.* ff. 112-13).

M. William Ryley B.Cn.L. 1422-1424.

By exch. Nov. 1422. D. before 19 May 1424 (*CPR. 1422-1429* p. 195).

M. William Pencrych Lic.C.L. ?-1434.

Occ. 1424 (Reg. Nicholls f. 41—in *Menevia Sacra* p. 178). Exch. archdcnry with William Thame for ch. of Edington, Wilts., 12 July 1434 (Salis., Reg. Neville pt. i f. 52b).

William Thame 1434-?

By exch. July 1434. Estate ratif. 23 Dec. 1441 (*CPR. 1441-1446* p. 31).

M. John Smith M.A. 1458.

Occ. 8 July 1458 (*CPL.* XI 179).

M. Richard Caunton D.Cn. & C.L. 1459.

Occ. 1459 (*Reg. J. Whethamstede,* ed. H. T. Riley (R.S. 28.6) I 336).

M. John Smith M.A. (again) 1473.

Occ. 22 June 1473 (*Reg. of R. Stillington and R. Fox,* ed. Sir H. C. Maxwell-Lyte (Somerset Record Soc., lii) p. 99).

M. John Hunden O.P., D.Th. 1476-1482.

Occ. 18 March 1476 (*CPL.* XIII ii 482). Res. 9 Aug. 1482[2] (*Reg. St Davids* II 451).

M. Dafydd Williams D.Cn.L. 1482-1492.

Coll. 9 Aug. 1482[2] (*Reg. St Davids* II 451). D. before 13 Feb. 1492 (*ibid.* p. 627).

John Denby 1492-?

Coll. 13 Feb. 1492 (*Reg. St Davids* II 627). Occ. 3 March 1496 (PCC 28 Horne).

---

[1] Bowland and Hiot appear to have exch. their benefices—archdcnry for the preb. of Caerfai, but no account is given of negotiations for this exch. (see p. 66).

[2] Hunden and Williams appear to have exch. benefices as Hunden was coll. 9 Aug. 1482 to the cursal preb. vac. by Williams (see p. 78) and Williams was coll. to the archdcnry s.d. There is no account of negotiations for this exch.

M. **John Hill** B.C.L. ?–1500.

D. as archdcn. before 7 Nov. 1500 (*Reg. St Davids* II 721).

M. **Thomas Saynte** D.C.L. 1500–1514.

Coll. 7 Nov. 1500 (*Reg. St Davids* II 721). D. before 6 Feb. 1514 (PCC 30 Fetiplace).

M. **John Fychan** D.C.L. ?–1527/8.

Occ. 17 Jan. 1518 (*Reg. St Davids* II 835). D. 4 Nov. 1527/1 July 1528 (PCC 34 Porch).

Andrew Whitmay O.Can.S.A. Bp. of Chrysopolis. ?–1547.[1]

Occ. 1529 (*L. & P.* IV iii No. 6047 p. 2701). Occ. 1535 (*Valor* IV 381). D. before Nov. 1547 (PCC 27 Alen).

ARCHDEACONS OF BRECON

Note: The prebend of Llanvaes was attached to this archdeaconry.

M. **Adam**[2] 1279, 1303.

Occ. 1 March 1279 (Brit. Mus., Harley MS. 6280 f. 61). Occ. 22 Feb. 1303 (*ibid.* f. 55b).

Philip ap Hywel 1328.

Occ. 21 Apr. 1328 (Cant., Reg. Q f. 166b).

M. **Gruffudd ap Rhys** 1345, 1366.

Occ. 9 Apr. 1345 (Brit. Mus., Harley MS. 6280 f. 42b). Occ. 16 Oct. 1366 (*Reg. Langham* p. 32).

Morgan ab Einion 1389–1408.

Adm. 26 March 1389 after royal gr. (Lamb., Reg. Courtenay f. 167b). He appears to have held the archdcnry previously as stated that had res. and been adm. again by royal gr. (*ibid.*). Occ. 16 Sept. 1402 (*Reg. St Davids* I 285). D. before 21 Apr. 1408[3] (*CPR. 1405–1408* p. 423).

Richard Gyldesford 1408.

Royal gr. 21 Apr. 1408 (*CPR. 1405–1408* p. 423). Adm. 23 Apr. (Lamb., Reg. Arundell 1 f. 319b).

Roger Stafford 1408–?

Adm. July 1408 by John Hiot, vicar general (Reg. Hiot f. 1b—in *Menevia Sacra* p. 194).

---

[1] Richard Fetherstone was said to have been archdcn. of St Davids c. 1534 (*Menevia Sacra* p. 182). Whitmay occ. as archdcn. 1529 and 1535 and held the benefice until his d., 1547, but it is possible that Fetherstone held it for a short period between 1529 and 13 Dec. 1534 when he was committed to the Tower. No evidence has been found for this. He was archdcn. of Brecon in 1529 and possibly confusion has arisen by his being styled 'an archdeacon in the church of St Davids' and this has been taken to mean St Davids itself rather than one of its four archdeaconries.

[2] He is called Adam Bareth by Le Neve-Hardy but no evidence has been found for this surname.

[3] The d. of Morgan ab Einion was commemorated in an inscription, now lost, in St Davids cath.: 'Petra, Precor die [dic?] Sic, Morganus ab Eyneon est hic' (*Menevia Sacra* p. 194).

M. **William Farrington** D.Th. 1410–?
William Chichele 1411.

Farrington coll. 14 Feb. 1410 (Reg. Hiot f. 4—in *Menevia Sacra* p. 194). Chichele occ. 10 Jan. 1411 (*CPL.* VI 214–15). Probably res. claims to archdcnry 1412 when preb. of Mathry. Farrington probably held archdcnry until d., before 20 June 1420 (Lincoln, Reg. XVI (Fleming) f. 147).

Robert Montgomery ?–1437.

Occ. 1421 (Reg. Nicholls f. 26—in *Menevia Sacra* p. 194). Res. before 26 March 1437 when obtained a cursal preb. (Reg. Rodburn f. 125—in *Menevia Sacra* p. 195).

M. **Llywellyn ap Madog** *or* **Lewis Rede** B.C.L. 1437.

Coll. 26 March 1437 (Reg. Rodburn f. 125—in *Menevia Sacra* p. 195). Res. before 16 July (Reg. Rodburn f. 126b—in *Menevia Sacra* p. 195).

Robert Cherberg 1437.

Coll. 16 July 1437 (Reg. Rodburn f. 126b—in *Menevia Sacra* p. 195). Res. before 12 Nov. (*ibid.*).

David Chirbury O.Carm. Bp. of Dromore. 1437–1452.
John Waldebeff 1452–?

Chirbury coll. 12 Nov. 1437 (Reg. Rodburn f. 126b—in *Menevia Sacra* p. 195). Gr. lic. 26 Feb. 1444 to exch. archdcnry for another benefice (*CPL.* IX 361–2). Held archdcnry until c. 20 Jan. 1452 when engaged in litigation with Waldebeff about possession (*ibid.* X 236). Waldebeff successful claimant (*ibid.*).

William ap Thomas 1481, 1497.

Occ. 7 Apr. 1481 (*CPL.* XIII ii 779). Occ. 26 Apr. 1497 (*Reg. St Davids* II 767).

M. **William Walter** D.Cn. & C.L. ?–1523.

Occ. 8 July 1504 (Lamb., Reg. Warham II f. 223). D. before 8 Apr. 1523 (*L. & P.* III ii No. 2992 (8)).

M. **Richard Fetherstone** M.A.[1] 1523–1534.

Royal gr. 8 Apr. 1523 (*L. & P.* III ii No. 2992 (8)). Occ. 1529 (*ibid.* IV iii No. 6047 p. 2701). Committed to the Tower 13 Dec. 1534 (*ibid.* VIII No. 1001).

M. **Richard Gwent** D.Cn.L. ?–1543/4.

Occ. 1 Aug. 1539 (Nat. Libr. Wales, SD Ch. B/1 p. 26). D. 21 July 1543/11 Feb. 1544 (PCC 3 Pynnyng).

ARCHDEACONS OF CARDIGAN

Note: The prebend of Llandyfriog was attached to this archdeaconry.

John Simons 1305.
Occ. 2 Apr. 1305 (Brit. Mus., Harley MS. 6280 f. 48).

Philip Fychan 1328.
Occ. 21 May 1328 (Cant., Reg. Q f. 166).[2]

---

[1] Fetherstone had been tutor to Princess Mary (*L. & P.* VIII No. 666 p. 251). He is called Dr Fetherstone July 1526 (*ibid.* IV i No. 2331 (2)), but there is no evidence that he obtained any further degree than M.A. (*Emden, Reg. Camb.* p. 226).

[2] There is no evidence that Fychan was archdcn. again 1354 as stated by Le Neve-Hardy.

M. Gruffudd Caunton[1] **1355, 1360.**
Occ. 8 Nov. 1355 (Brit. Mus., Harley MS. 6280 ff. 49–49b). Occ. 28 Nov. 1360 (*ibid.* f. 45b).

M. Philip de Caunton 1368.
Occ. 28 July 1368 (Brit. Mus., Harley MS. 6280 f. 19).

Richard de Caunton ?–1401.
Occ. 8 June 1383 (*Reg. St Davids* II 629). Estate ratif. 9 Nov. 1390 (*CPR. 1388–1392* p. 198) and 19 Sept. 1394 (*CPR. 1391–1396* p. 481). D. before 31 March 1401 (*Reg. St Davids* I 207).

M. John Colle Sch.C.L. 1401–1407.
Coll. 31 March 1401 (*Reg. St Davids* I 207). Chancellor 1407.

Henry Gardiner 1407.
Coll. 21 Jan. 1407 (*Reg. St Davids* I 379). Res. or d. before 21 Nov. (*ibid.* II 407).

Roger de Bottal 1407–?
Royal gr. 15 Dec. 1407 (*CPR. 1405–1408* p. 383). Coll. 18 Jan. 1408 (*Reg. St Davids* II 409).

Nicholas Clifton ?–1420.
D. as archdcn. before 14 July 1420 (Reg. Nicholls f. 32—in *Menevia Sacra* p. 223).

M. William Canon 1420–1425.
Coll. 14 July 1420 (Reg. Nicholls f. 32—in *Menevia Sacra* p. 223). Exch. archdcnry with John Turbot for ch. of Mersham, Kent, 25 Feb. 1425 (*Reg. Chichele* I 224).

John Turbot 1425–?
By exch. Feb. 1425. Occ. 1426 (Reg. Nicholls f. 47—in *Menevia Sacra* p. 223).

M. John ap Rhys D.C.L. 1432, 1439.
Occ. 28 Apr. 1432 (Brit. Mus., Harley MS. 1249 f. 281). Occ. 1439 (Reg. Rodburn f. 111—in *Menevia Sacra* p. 223).

M. Richard Caunton D.C.L. 1446.
Occ. 8 Nov. 1446 (P.R.O., C 84/46/41).

John William[2] **1458.**
Occ. 27 May 1458 (*Reg. Bourgchier* p. 242).

M. Lewis Owain ab Owain D.Cn.L. ?–1487.
Occ. 9 Feb. 1476 (*CPL.* XIII ii 496). D. before 29 Aug. 1487 (*Reg. St Davids* II 505).

M. Thomas ap Hywel 1487–?
Coll. 29 Aug. 1487 (*Reg. St Davids* II 505). Occ. 2 March 1512 (PCC 30 Fetiplace).

John Luntley ?–1542.
Occ. 1529 (*L. & P.* IV iii No. 6047 p. 2701). D. before 17 Nov. 1542 (PCC 13 Spert).

---

[1] There is no evidence that Howel ap Griffith (Hywel ap Gruffudd) held the archdcnry 1331 as stated by Le Neve-Hardy.

[2] William is said to have obtained the archdcnry by exch. with Maurice Winter for ch. of Llandyssul, Card, 16 July 1454 (*Menevia Sacra* p. 223—authority of Browne Willis MS. collections).

ARCHDEACONS OF CARMARTHEN

Note: The prebend of Llanrhian was attached to this archdeaconry.

Walter Winter[1] 1328, 1330.
Occ. 21 Apr. 1328 (Cant., Reg. Q f. 163). Occ. 28 Jan. 1330 (Brit. Mus., Harley MS. 6280 f. 62b).

M. Gruffudd Caunton ?–1355/6.[2]
Occ. 14 Feb. 1335 (Brit. Mus., Harley MS. 6280 f. 58b). Res. before 22 Nov. 1356 (*CPR. 1354–1358* p. 477).

M. Hywel ap Dafydd Fychan Sch. Cn. & C.L. 1356–?
M. David Martin of Rosemarket B.C.L. 1357–?
John Clyewe 1359–?
Royal gr. to Hywel 22 Nov. 1356 (*CPR. 1354–1358* p. 477). Martin prov. 18 July 1357 (*CPL.* III 581). Papal mand. 20 July to adm. Hywel if found fit in Latin although he had obtained archdcnry in ignorance that it had been reserved to pope during lifetime of Caunton, previous archdcn. (*ibid.*). Royal gr. to Clyewe 18 Oct. 1359 (*CPR. 1358–1361* p. 301). Martin engaged in litigation about archdcnry, stated 24 Aug. 1360 that had obtained three sentences in his favour, but that Hywel had d. before he could execute judgt. (*CPP.* I 316). Martin petitioned s.d. for rights of Hywel in archdcnry (*ibid.* p. 358). Clyewe appears to have res. claims since Martin occ. as archdcn. 30 Jan. 1361 (*ibid.* p. 365).

William Baldwin 1368.
Estate ratif. 29 May 1368 (*CPR. 1367–1370* p. 121).

William Nicholls 1383, 1389.
M. John David 1386.
Nicholls occ. 14 Dec. 1383 (*CPR. 1381–1385* p. 345). David occ. 7 March 1386 (*CCR. 1385–1389* p. 57). Nicholls occ. 6 Apr. 1389 (Lamb., Reg. Courtenay f. 167).

M. Edmund Warham Lic.Cn.L. 1391–?
Royal gr. 28 Aug. 1391 (*CPR. 1388–1392* p. 478). Occ. 16 Sept. 1402 (*Reg. St Davids* I 285).

John Walton ?–1404.
D. as archdcn. before 18 Aug. 1404 (*CPL.* VI 44–5).

M. Adam de Usk D.C.L. 1404–?
Prov. 18 Aug. 1404 (*CPL.* VI 44–5).

William Chichele 1408–?
Coll. 1408 (Reg. Chichele f. 2b—in *Menevia Sacra* p. 208). ? Held archdcnry until 1412 when preb. of Mathry.

M. William Newport B.C.L. 1412–?
Obtained archdcnry by exch. with unnamed person for archdcnry of Salop c. 1412 (*CPL.* VII 53–4). Occ. 16 Nov. 1417 (*Reg. Chichele* II 134).[3]

---

[1] Gilbert de Mossylwicke is said to have been archdcn. 1300, 1313 (*Menevia Sacra* p. 207—authority of Browne Willis MS. collections).

[2] Caunton possibly res. the archdcnry of Carmarthen 1355 since he occ. as archdcn. of Cardigan in that year. His res. is only mentioned 22 Nov. 1356 when his successor was collated.

[3] Newport is said to have been cited to convocation as archdcn. 1421, 1424, 1426 (*Menevia Sacra* p. 208—no reference given).

William Pirrye 1432, 1439.

Occ. 28 Apr. 1432 (Brit. Mus., Harley MS. 1249 f. 281). Occ. 1439 (Reg. Rodburn f. 111b—in *Menevia Sacra* p. 208).

M. Richard Keyr[1] ?–1488.

Occ. 10 Dec. 1482 (*Reg. St Davids* II 455). D. 7 June/4 July 1488[2] (*ibid*. p. 533).

M. John Morgan *or* **Young** B.Cn.L. 1488–1494.

Coll. 4 July 1488 (*Reg. St Davids* II 533). Res. before 13 Feb. 1494 (*ibid*. p. 677).

M. Henry ap Hywel 1494–1509.

Coll. 13 Feb. 1494 (*Reg. St Davids* II 677). D. before 28 May 1509 (*L. & P.* I i No. 94 (26)).

Edward ap John 1509–?

Royal gr. 6 June 1509 (*L. & P.* I i No. 94 (26)). Occ. 1529 (*ibid*. IV iii No. 6047 p. 2701).

M. Gruffudd Leyshon D.C.L. 1535, 1560.

Occ. 1535 (*Valor* IV 383). Occ. 1560 (Nat. Libr. Wales, SD Ch. B/1 p. 26).

PREBENDARIES OF BRAWDY

John Goch 1347–1348.

Royal gr. 27 Feb. 1347 (*CPR. 1345–1348* p. 268). Preb. had been appropriated to the bishop's table for fifty years and more, but had been appropriated without royal lic., therefore k. gr. preb. to Goch (*CPR. 1348–1350* p. 26). Appropriation of preb. by bp. conf. by k. 12 Feb. 1348 and gr. to Goch revoked (*ibid*.).

PREBENDARIES OF CAERFAI

William de Osberton ?–1360.

Prov. to canonry with reservn. of preb. 22 Oct. 1343 (*CPP.* I 24). Exch. preb. of Caerfai with Thomas David for ch. of Shalfleet, Isle of Wight, Hants, 10 June 1360 (Winchester, Reg. Edington I f. 100).

M. Thomas David 1360–1361.

By exch. June 1360. Mand. adm. 26 June (Winchester, Reg. Edington I f. 100). D. before 21 June 1361 (*CPP.* I 318).

Dafydd Fychan 1361–?
John de Saxton 1361–1363.

Fychan prov. 21 June 1361 (*CPP.* I 318). Royal gr. to Saxton 30 July (*CPR. 1361–1364* p. 44). Retained possession as exch. preb. with Robert de Congham for preb. of Sandiacre, Lichfield, 18 Nov. 1363 (Lichfield, Reg. IV (Stretton) f. 55).

Robert de Congham 1363–?

By exch. Nov. 1363. Occ. July 1366 (*Reg. Sudbury* II 159).

---

[1] Geoffrey Caunton is said to have been archdcn. 1470 (*Menevia Sacra* p. 28—authority Browne Willis MS. collections).

[2] The d. of one Robert Keir, arcdcn. of Carmarthen, is recorded on 27 June 1488 in a series of Welsh obits (Cambridge, Trinity College MS. 224 f. 1). This is presumably the same man.

John de Bowland ?–1389.[1]
Res. this preb. before 20 Feb. 1389 (*CPR. 1388–1392* p. 7).

Walter Almaly 1389.
Royal gr. 20 Feb. 1389 (*CPR. 1388–1392* p. 7). D. before 12 Sept. (*ibid.* p. 103).

M. John Hiot ?–1400.
Occ. 15 Oct. 1397 (*CPR. 1396–1399* p. 218). Archdcn. of St Davids 1400.[2]

John de Bowland (again) 1400.[2]
Coll. 24 June 1400 (*Reg. St Davids* I 175). D. before 4 Dec. (*ibid.* p. 195).

Robert Tunstall 1400–?
Coll. 4 Dec. 1400 (*Reg. St Davids* I 195).

William Hawkesworth 1426.
Occ. 1426 (Reg. Nicholls f. 49b—in *Menevia Sacra* p. 282).

William Thame 1436–?
Coll. 8 July 1436 (Reg. Rodburn, no f. given—in *Menevia Sacra* p. 282).

Richard Carswell 1504.
Occ. 8 July 1504 (Lamb., Reg. Warham II f. 223).

M. William Vennor 1539.
Occ. 1 Aug. 1539 (Nat. Libr. Wales, SD Ch. B/1 p. 26).

M. Stephen Grene 1541.
Occ. 1 Aug. 1541 (Nat. Libr. Wales, SD Ch. B/1 p. 28). ? Held preb. until d., 1 March/29 Nov. 1549 (PCC 60 Chaynay).

PREBENDARIES OF CAERFARCHELL

John Godmeston.
Occ. as can. of St Davids 24 Nov. 1393 (Lamb., Reg. Arundell I ff. 160–160b). Held preb. of Caerfarchell before Ralph Repynton (Lichfield, Reg. VI (Scrope) f. 72b; see below).

Ralph Repynton ?–1396.
Exch. this preb. and the preb. of Wartling, Ninfield and Hooe, Hastings royal free chap., Suss., with Nicholas Mockyng for deanery of St Chad's colleg. ch., Shrewsbury, Salop, 27 July 1396 (Lichfield, Reg. VI (Scrope) f. 72b).

M. Nicholas Mockyng B.C.L. 1396–?
By exch. July 1396. Occ. 18 Aug. 1411 (*CPL.* VI 292).[3]

Henry Shalston ?–1486.
Res. this preb. before 27 Jan. 1486 (*Reg. St Davids* II 461).

---

[1] Bowland probably res. this preb. in 1388 as he occ. as archdcn. of St Davids that year, but his successor was not coll. to Caerfai until 1389.

[2] Hiot and Bowland appear to have exch. their benefices, preb. of Caerfai and archdcnry of St Davids, but there is no account of any transactions for such an exch. (see p. 60).

[3] The preb. held by Mockyng Aug. 1411 is called the preb. 'Siuenonune' (*CPL.* VI 292). This has been interpreted as the nameless preb.—'sine nomine'. This may imply that Mockyng had res. Caerfarchell at this date and held a cursal preb. in St Davids, but possibly the name of the preb. was omitted in a letter to the curia, which would have led the clerks of the curia to assume that his preb. had no name.

M. **Lewis ap John** B.Cn. & C.L. 1486–1487.
Coll. 27 Jan. 1486 (*Reg. St Davids* II 461). Chancellor 1487.

M. **William Nele** M.A. 1487–?
Coll. 29 Dec. 1487 (*Reg. St Davids* II 513). Occ. 8 July 1504 (Lamb., Reg. Warham II f. 223). ? Held preb. until d., 8 Aug. 1509 (*Worcs. Archaeol. Soc. Trans.* iii (1925–6) 119–20).

Morgan Lewis ?–1554.
Occ. 1535 (*Valor* IV 383). D. before 25 July 1554 (Nat. Libr. Wales, SD/BR/2 f. 6).

PREBENDARIES OF CLYDEY

Richard Garland 1354, 1366.
Prov. to canonry with reservn. of preb. 22 Apr. 1353 (*CPL.* III 497). Estate ratif. as preb. of Clydey 6 Nov. 1354 (*CPR. 1354–1358* p. 131). Occ. June 1366 (*Reg. Sudbury* II 155).

Hugh atte Halle 1375.
Estate ratif. 28 June 1375 (*CPR. 1374–1377* p. 122).

M. **Thomas Picton** ?–1403.
D. as preb. before 29 Oct. 1403 (*Reg. St Davids* I 301).

M. **Robert Raulyn** B.Cn.L. 1403–?
Coll. 29 Oct. 1403 (*Reg. St Davids* I 301). Probably held preb. until d., 5/20 Feb. 1417 because then called preb. of St Davids (*Reg. Chichele* II 110–12).

Robert Merflete ?–1426.
Occ. as can. 16 Nov. 1417 (*Reg. Chichele* I 134). Exch. preb. of Clydey with Richard Newport for preb. in St John's colleg. ch., Chester, 21 Oct./14 Nov. 1426 (Lichfield, Reg. IX (Heyworth) ff. 116b–117; Reg. Nicholls f. 51—in *Menevia Sacra* pp. 245–6).

Richard Newport 1426–1434.
By exch. Oct./Nov. 1426. Res. 30 June 1434 when obtained a cursal preb. (Reg. Rodburn ff. 103, 106—in *Menevia Sacra* p. 246).

M. **John de la Bere** B.Cn.L. 1434–1447.
Coll. 30 June 1434 (Reg. Rodburn ff. 103, 106—in *Menevia Sacra* p. 246). Bp. of St Davids 1447.

John Wigmour ?–1502.
Depriv. before 15 Nov. 1502 (*Reg. St Davids* II 747).

Lewis ap Rhys 1502–?
Coll. 15 Nov. 1502 (*Reg. St Davids* II 747).

M. **William Fychan** D.C.L. ?–1517.
Res. this preb. before 18 Apr. 1517 when preb. of Mathry (*Reg. St Davids* II 814).

M. **Maurice Gwyn** B.Th. 1517–?
Coll. 18 Apr. 1517 (*Reg. St Davids* II 814).

John Spendlove ?–1554.
Occ. 1535 (*Valor* IV 383). Depriv. before 21 July 1554 (Nat. Libr. Wales, SD/BR/2 f. 5).

PREBENDARIES OF LAMPETER-PONT-STEPHEN

The prebend of Lampeter-pont-Stephen was attached to the precentorship.

PREBENDARIES OF LLANDDEWI-ABERARTH

M. Richard de la Barre Sch.C.L. 1366.
Prov. 6 July 1343 to an unnamed preb. in St Davids (*CPP.* I 64). Occ. as preb. of Llanddewi-Aberarth 18 Oct. 1366 (*Reg. Langham* p. 32).[1]

M. John de Lincoln Sch.Cn.L. 1397, 1399.
Estate ratif. 25 May 1397 (*CPR. 1396–1399* p. 139) and 22 Oct. 1399 (*CPR. 1399–1401* pp. 24–5).

William Wilcock[2] ?–1502.
Occ. 16 Apr. 1501 (Brit. Mus., Harley MS. 1249 f. 272). D. before 20 July 1502 (*Reg. St Davids* II 739).

M. John Fychan D.C.L. 1502–?
Coll. 29 Sept. 1502 (*Reg. St Davids* II 745). Occ. 8 July 1504 (Lamb., Reg. Warham II f. 223).

M. Richard Gwent D.Cn.L. 1535, 1539.
Occ. 1535 (*Valor* IV 383). Occ. 1 Aug. 1539 (Nat. Libr. Wales, SD Ch. B/1 p. 26). ? Held preb. until d., 21 July 1543/11 Feb. 1544 (PCC 3 Pynnyng).

PREBENDARIES OF LLANDYFRIOG

The prebend of Llandyfriog was attached to the archdeaconry of Cardigan.

PREBENDARIES OF LLANDYSSILIO-GOGO

The prebend of Llandyssilio-gogo was attached to the treasurership.

PREBENDARIES OF LLANGAN

Robert de Whitney 1366.
Prov. to an unnamed preb. in St Davids 9 Aug. 1343 (*CPP.* I 70). Occ. as preb. of Llangan 18 Oct. 1366 (*Reg. Langham* p. 33).

[1] Robert Mason, Thomas Donclent, John Sampson, John de Middleton and Philip Davy, who are given as prebs. of Llanddewi-Aberarth (*Menevia Sacra* pp. 268–9) are not included here. Evidence shows that it was in a cursal preb. that the succession from Donclent to Davy took place. See p. 75.

[2] There is no evidence that William Eliot held this preb. 1488 and 1493 (*Menevia Sacra* p. 269, no reference given).

Walter de Brugge ?–1396.

Exch. this preb., ch. of Burwell, Cambs., and free chap. of Watton at Stone, Herts., with Thomas Sprot for archdcnry of Meath, Ireland, 14 March/3 Apr. 1396 (Norwich, Reg. Despenser ff. 210b–211; Lincoln, Reg. XI (Buckingham) f. 281b).

M. Thomas Sprot B.C.L. 1396–?

By exch. March/Apr. 1396.

M. Andrew Holes Lic.Cn.L. 1436–1438.[1]

Coll. 10 Feb. 1436 (Reg. Rodburn f. 107—in *Menevia Sacra* p. 262). Preb. of Mathry 1438.

Nicholas Wymbyssh 1438–?

Coll. 22 July 1438 (Reg. Rodburn f. 107—in *Menevia Sacra* p. 262). ? Held preb. until d., before 30 Jan. 1461 (York, Reg. W. Booth f. 51b).

M. John Bell ?–1492.

Occ. as can. 3 Nov. 1478 (*CPL.* XIII ii 627). D. as preb. of Llangan before 6 Jan. 1492 (*Reg. St Davids* II 633).

William Wilcock 1492–1502.

Coll. 6 Jan. 1492 (*Reg. St Davids* II 633). D. before 20 July 1502 (*ibid.* p. 739).

Geoffrey Hywel 1504.

Occ. 8 July 1504 (Lamb., Reg. Warham II f. 223).

M. William Atwater D.Th. ?–1514.

Res. this preb. 1514 when bp. of Lincoln (*Reg. St Davids* II 809).

M. Maurice Adams B.Cn.L. 1514–?

Coll. 25 Nov. 1514 (*Reg. St Davids* II 809).

M. Richard Rawlings 1535.[2]

Occ. 1535 (*Valor* IV 383).

M. Richard Gwent D.Cn.L. 1541.[2]

Occ. 1 Aug. 1541 (Nat. Libr. Wales, SD Ch. B/1 p. 28). ? Held preb. until d., 21 July 1543/11 Feb. 1544 (PCC 3 Pynnyng).

PREBENDARIES OF LLANRHIAN

The prebend of Llanrhian was attached to the archdeaconry of Carmarthen.

PREBENDARIES OF LLANVAES

The prebend of Llanvaes was attached to the archdeaconry of Brecon.

---

[1] John Barry is said to have been preb. of Llangan 1406 (*Menevia Sacra* p. 262—authority Browne Willis MS. collections). John Colle and John Scot who are also given as prebs. of Llangan, following Barry, have not been included here as the evidence is insufficient. 'John Cole is said to have been collated Prebendary of Llangan 21 Jan. 1406, though I find not this in ye Register' (*ibid.*). There is similarly no evidence for the collation of John Scot in succession to Colle (*ibid.*).

[2] Richard Smithe, described as 'parson of Llangan', was imprisoned for treasonable words 23 Feb. 1540 (*L. & P.* xv No. 252 (2)). It has been suggested that Smithe could have been an alias for Rawlings or Gwent (*ibid.* n.).

PREBENDARIES OF LLAWHADEN

The prebend of Llawhaden was attached to the chancellorship.

PREBENDARIES OF MATHRY

M. Adam de Houghton D.C.L. 1356–1361.
Royal gr. 10 Nov. 1356 (*Cal. Ch. Rolls 1341–1417* p. 149)—called de Henton. Res. Sept. 1361 when bp. of St. Davids.

John de Buckingham 1361–1362.
Philip de Houghton 1361.
Royal gr. to Buckingham 28 Oct. 1361 (*CPR. 1361–1364* p. 101). Houghton prov. 25 Nov. (*CPP.* I 280). Probably did not obtain possession because Buckingham vac. an unnamed preb. in St Davids, probably Mathry, 1362 when bp. of Lincoln (*CPL.* IV 87).

Henry de Snaith ?–1376.
Occ. July 1366 (*Reg. Sudbury* II 167). Exch. this preb. and preb. of Henfield, Chichester, with John de Fordham for preb. of North Newbald, York, 9 May 1376 (York, Reg. A. Neville I f. 4).

John de Fordham 1376–1381.
By exch. May 1376. Bp. of Durham 1381.

Louis Donati O.F.M., Card. pr. of S. Marcus. ?–1386.
Occ. 20 Nov. 1384 (*Cal. Anct. Correspondence* p. 196). D. Dec. 1386 (*Eubel* I 44).

Alan Leverton 1388.
Royal gr. 12 March 1388 (*CPR. 1385–1389* p. 416).

William de Cotyngham 1388–?
Royal gr. 24 Nov. 1388 (*CPR. 1385–1388* p. 528).

M. Thomas More 1389–?
Royal gr. 17 Feb. 1389 (*CPR. 1388–1392* p. 12). Adm. 3 March (Lamb., Reg. Courtenay f. 167b).[1]

John Haywood ?–1412.
D. as preb. before 18 March 1412 (Reg. Chichele f. 11—in *Menevia Sacra* p. 235).

William Chichele 1412–1424.
Coll. 18 March 1412 (Reg. Chichele f. 11—in *Menevia Sacra* p. 235). D. before 10 June 1424 (*Reg. Chichele* I 240).

Edmund Nicholls 1425–1426.
Prov. 16 Nov. 1425 (*CPL.* VII 401). Res. before 8 June 1426 (Reg. Nicholls, no f. given—in *Menevia Sacra* p. 236).

M. John Carpenter B.Th. 1426–1431.
Coll. 8 June 1426 (Reg. Nicholls, no f. given—in *Menevia Sacra* p. 236). Exch.

---

[1] More possibly held the preb. of Mathry again for a short time before his d., 7 Feb. 1420/26 Dec. 1421 since he is called preb. of St Davids in his will and bequeathed 4s to the prebendal ch. of Mathry (*Reg. Chichele* II 230–4).

preb. with Dafydd ap Rhys for a cursal preb. and the preb of Clifton, Lincoln, 7 Sept. 1431[1] (Reg. Nicholls f. 75—in *Menevia Sacra* pp. 237, 309).

M. Dafydd ap Rhys D.C.L. 1431–1438.
By exch. Sept. 1431. D. before 22 July 1438 (Reg. Rodburn f. 123b—in *Menevia Sacra* p. 237).

M. Andrew Holes Lic.Cn.L. 1438–1446.
Coll. 22 July 1438 (Reg. Rodburn f. 123b—in *Menevia Sacra* p. 237). Exch. preb. with Robert Stillington for preb. of Eastharptree, Wells, 3 Feb. 1446 (*Reg. of T. Bekynton*, ed. Sir H. C. Maxwell-Lyte and M. C. B. Dawes (Somerset Record Soc., xlix, l) 1 58).

M. Robert Stillington D.C.L. 1446–1465.
By exch. Feb. 1446. Bp. of Bath and Wells 1465.

William Wall 1496–?
Royal gr. 15 Apr. 1496 (*CPR. 1494–1509* p. 45).

M. Griffin Padarn B.C.L. 1504.
Occ. 8 July 1504 (Lamb., Reg. Warham II f. 223).

M. Robert Chapel D.Th. ?–1517.
D. as preb. before 18 Apr. 1517 (*Reg. St Davids* II 814).

M. William Fychan D.C.L. 1517–?
Coll. 18 Apr. 1517 (*Reg. St Davids* II 814). Occ. 1 Aug. 1539 (Nat. Libr. Wales, SD Ch. B/1 p. 26).

M. Thomas Barlow 1541.
Occ. 1 Aug. 1541 (Nat. Libr. Wales, SD Ch. B/1 p. 28).

PREBENDARIES OF MYDRIM

The prebend of Mydrim was attached to the archdeaconry of St Davids.

PREBENDARIES OF ST NICHOLAS PENFFOES

John Bodilly 1389–?
Royal gr. 3 July 1389 (*CPR. 1388–1392* p. 72).

John Godmeston ?–1396.
Estate ratif. 27 Nov. 1396 (*CPR. 1396–1399* p. 40). Exch. this preb. and preb. of Boughrood, Abergwili colleg. ch., Carm., with Nicholas Hereford for chancellorship of St Paul's cath., London, 13 Dec. (Lond., Guildhall, Reg. Braybroke f. 148).

M. Nicholas Hereford D.Th. 1396–1397.
By exch. Dec. 1396. Adm. 17 Dec. (Lond., Guildhall, Reg. Braybroke f. 148). Exch. preb. with Robert de Wermyngton for ch. of Somerton, Oxon., 12/15 Aug. 1397 (Lincoln, Reg. XI (Buckingham) ff. 337–337b; *CPR. 1396–1399* p. 186).

---

[1] This exch. is not mentioned in the Lincoln register, but Dafydd ap Rhys was succeeded by Carpenter as preb. of Clifton 1431.

Robert de Wermyngton 1397–1399.

By exch. Aug. 1397. Adm. 18 Aug. (Lamb., Reg. Arundell I f. 456b). Estate ratif. 31 Oct. 1399 (*CPR. 1399–1401* p. 55). Exch. preb. with John Launce for free chap. of Tothill, Westminster, 12 Nov. (*Reg. St Davids* I 137–9).

M. John Launce B.C.L. 1399–?
John Haywood 1405–1406.

Launce obtained preb. by exch. Nov. 1399. Adm. 22 Nov. (*Reg. St Davids* I 139). Haywood prov. 2 Feb. 1405 (*CPL.* VI 43). Gr. royal lic. 7 Sept. to execute prov. (*CPR. 1405–1408* p. 49). Estate ratif. 22 Nov. (*ibid.* p. 91). Royal gr. 5 and 27 March 1406 (*ibid.* p. 158; *Reg. St Davids* I 339). Judgt. given in chancery in favour of Launce, mand. to restore to preb. 30 June (*CPR. 1405–1408* p. 194). Gr. to Haywood revoked s.d. (*ibid.*). Estate of Launce ratif. 19 Feb. 1407 (*ibid.* p. 244).

William Hodenet ?–1431.

Exch. this preb. with Richard Hoore for preb. in St Crantock's colleg. ch., Cornw., 18 July/Aug. 1431 (Reg. Nicholls f. 74—in *Menevia Sacra* p. 256; Exeter, Reg. Lacy I f. 105b).

M. Richard Hoore 1431–1437.

By exch. July/Aug. 1431. Exch. preb. with John Blodwel for preb. of Combe Septima, Wells, 10 March 1437 (*Reg. of J. Stafford, bishop of Bath and Wells*, ed. T. S. Holmes (Somerset Record Soc., xxxi, xxxii) II 203).

M. John Blodwel D.Cn.L. 1437–?

By exch. March 1437. ? Held preb. until d., 13 Apr. 1462 (*Emden, Reg. Ox.* I 203).

M. Richard Rhaidr[1] D.C.L. 1497–?

Coll. 20 Apr. 1497 (*Reg. St Davids* I 737). Occ. 8 July 1504 (Lamb., Reg. Warham II f. 223).

Lewis Gwyn 1535.
Occ. 1535 (*Valor* IV 383).

Thomas Hogeson 1539, 1541.
Occ. 1 Aug. 1539 and 1 Aug. 1541 (Nat. Libr. Wales, SD Ch. B/1 pp. 26, 28).

PREBENDARIES OF TREFLODEN

M. Alexander King ?–1487.
D. as preb. before 4 May 1487 (*Reg. St Davids* II 499).

M. William Eliot B.C.L. 1487–?
Coll. 4 May 1487 (*Reg. St Davids* II 499).

M. Richard Hill B.Cn.L. ?–1489.
Res. this preb. 1489 when bp. of London (*Reg. St Davids* II 579).

M. Richard Geffrey B.Cn.L. 1489–1490.
Coll. 9 Dec. 1489 (*Reg. St Davids* II 579). D. before 5 Aug. 1490 (*ibid.* p. 597).

M. John Barret M.A. 1490–?
Coll. 5 Aug. 1490 (*Reg. St Davids* II 597). Held unnamed preb. 20 July 1493 (*ibid.* p. 661).

[1] William Wilcock is said to have been preb. of St Nicholas Penffoes 1490 (*Menevia Sacra* p. 256—no reference given).

M. John Gruffudd 1504.

Occ. 8 July 1504 (Lamb., Reg. Warham II f. 223). ? Held preb. until d., 3 Apr./2 May 1523 (PCC 8 Bodfelde).

CURSAL PREBENDARIES OF ST DAVIDS

The endowment of the six cursal prebends of St Davids consisted of the tithes of the parishes of St Davids and Whitchurch in Dewsland; the parishes were divided into cylchau, each cylch was divided into portions and the tithes of the portions were apportioned annually by lot to the different prebendaries, with the exception of the archdeacon of Cardigan, whose prebend always remained fixed on Cylch Gwaelod y Wlad. The endowment of the prebends circulated from cylch to cylch and the portions in question were called cursal prebends, as a result of this system. The names of the prebendaries have been listed in chronological order, from the dates of collation or first occurrence, because the individual cursal prebends do not appear, from the evidence of contemporary sources, ever to have been distinguished by any name or number (see appendix pp. 86–7).

M. Thomas Donclent Lic.Cn. & C.L. ?–1388.

Occ. as can. and preb. 1362 (Lamb., Reg. Wittlesey f. 10). Vac. a cursal preb. before 2 Oct. 1388 (*CPR. 1385–1389* p. 515). Succeeded by John Sampson (see below p. 74).

M. Michael Haynton Lic.Th. ?–1366.

Vac. preb. before 9 Oct. 1366 (Lincoln, Reg. XII (Buckingham) f. 45). Succeeded by Geoffrey Salyng (see below).

M. Geoffrey Salyng D.C.L. 1366.

Prov. to canonry with reservn. of preb. 26 Apr. 1363 (*CPP.* I 417). Occ. as cursal preb. 9 and 12 Oct. 1366, then holding preb. vac. by Michael Haynton (Lincoln, Reg. XII (Buckingham) f. 45; *Reg. Langham* p. 55; see above).

Samuel de Wyk[1] 1384.

Occ. 20 Nov. 1384 (*Cal. Anct. Correspondence* p. 196).

M. John Abraham ?–1387.

Vac. preb. before 17 Dec. 1387 (*CPR. 1385–1389* p. 378). Succeeded by Samuel de Wyk (see below).

Samuel de Wyk ?–1394.

Estate ratif. 17 Dec. 1387 in preb. vac. by John Abraham (*CPR. 1385–1389* p. 378; see above). Exch. preb. with Thomas Guldesfeld for ch. of English Bicknor, Glos., 9 Sept. 1394 (*Reg. Trefnant* p. 189; see below p. 74).

M. Richard Bokulton ?–1388.

Vac. preb. before 1 Oct. 1388 (*CPR. 1385–1389* p. 509). Succeeded by John Hiot (see below).

M. John Hiot 1388–1397.

Estate ratif. 1 Oct. 1388 in preb. vac. by Richard Bokulton (*CPR. 1385–1389* p. 509; see above). Royal gr. 14 June 1389 (*CPR. 1388–1392* p. 47). Adm. 21 June (Lamb., Reg. Courtenay f. 273b). Preb. of Caerfai 1397.

[1] Wyk is described as 'an alien staying in England' (*Cal. Anct. Correspondence* p. 196).

John Sampson 1388–1397.

Estate ratif. 2 Oct. 1388 in preb. vac. by Thomas Donclent (*CPR. 1385–1389* p. 515; see above p. 73). Royal gr. 14 June 1389 (*CPR. 1388–1392* p. 45). Adm. 21 June (Lamb., Reg. Courtenay f. 273b). D. before 11 Sept. 1397 (*CPR. 1396–1399* p. 189). Succeeded by John de Middleton (see below p. 75).

M. William Polgrim ?–1388.

Vac. preb. before 2 Oct. 1388 (*CPR. 1385–1389* p. 515). Succeeded by Gilbert Nicholls (see below).

Gilbert Nicholls 1388–1398.

Estate ratif. 2 Oct. 1388 in preb. vac. by William Polgrim (*CPR. 1385–1389* p. 515; see above). Royal gr. 15 June 1389 (*CPR. 1388–1392* p. 51). Adm. 21 June (Lamb., Reg. Courtenay f. 273b). D. before 31 July 1398 (*Reg. St Davids* I 67). Succeeded by Thomas Ayleward (see below p. 75).

M. John de Sweyveseye[1] B.Cn.L. ?–1389.

Vac. preb. before 1 March 1389 (*CPR. 1388–1392* p. 18). Succeeded by Walter de Brugge (see below).

Walter de Brugge 1389.

Royal gr. 1 March 1389 of preb. vac. by John de Sweyveseye (*CPR. 1388–1392* p. 18; see above). Vac. preb. before 19 Aug.[2] (*CPR. 1388–1392* p. 101). Succeeded by Matthew de Hanemere (see below).

Roger Nassh ?–1389.

D. as preb. before 6 March 1389 (*CPR. 1388–1392* p. 38). Succeeded by John Porter (see below).

John Porter 1389–1402.

Estate ratif. 6 March 1389 in preb. vac. by Roger Nassh (*CPR. 1388–1392* p. 38; see above). Res. before 4 Aug. 1402 (*Reg. St Davids* I 263). Succeeded by John David (see below p. 75).

M. Matthew de Hanemere D.C.L. 1389, 1390.

Estate ratif. 19 Aug. 1389 and 26 July 1390 in preb. vac. by John de Sweyveseye (*CPR. 1388–1392* pp. 101, 295; see above).

Hugh le Yonge

Held cursal preb. n.d., succeeded by Walter de Brugge (Norwich, Reg. Despenser f. 191b; see below).

Walter de Brugge ?–1394.

Exch. preb. vac. by Hugh le Yonge (see above) with Richard Petir for an unnamed benefice in Norwich dioc.,[3] 16 June 1394 (Norwich, Reg. Despenser f. 191b; see below).

Richard Petir 1394–1406.

By exch. with Walter de Brugge for an unnamed benefice in Norwich dioc.,[3] 16 June 1394 (Norwich, Reg. Despenser f. 191b; see above). Res. before 25 Jan. 1406 (*CPL.* VI 85). Succeeded by Thomas Tholite (see below p. 75).

Thomas Guldesfeld 1394–1408.

By exch. with Samuel de Wyk for ch. of English Bicknor, Glos., 9 Sept. 1394

---

[1] John de Sweyveseye was of Swavesey, Cambs., not of Swansea, Glam.

[2] Walter de Brugge possibly obtained the preb. of Llangan in 1389 (see p. 69).

[3] This benefice was probably the ch. of Burwell, Cambs. (see p. 69).

(*Reg. Trefnant* p. 189; see above p. 73). Res. before 25 Jan. 1408 (Reg. Hiot f. 2—in *Menevia Sacra* p. 304). Succeeded by Robert Burgeys (see below p. 76).

M. John de Middleton M.A. 1397–?

Royal gr. 11 Sept. 1397 of preb. vac. by John Sampson (*CPR. 1396–1399* p. 189; see above p. 74). Mand. adm. 25 Sept. (Lamb., Reg. Arundell 1 f. 457). Estate ratif. 27 Oct. 1399 (*CPR. 1399–1401* p. 25).[1]

Thomas Ayleward 1398–1413.

Coll. 31 July 1398 to preb. vac. by Gilbert Nicholls (*Reg. St Davids* 1 67; see above p. 74). D. before 1 May 1413 (Reg. Chichele f. 12—in *Menevia Sacra* p. 287). Succeeded by Roger atte Herne (see below p. 76).

M. Nicholas Hethe B.C.L. ?–1398.

Vac. preb. before 14 Aug. 1398 (*Reg. St Davids* 1 71–3). Succeeded by John Haywood (see below).

John Haywood 1398–1405.

Coll. 14 Aug. 1398 to preb. vac. by Nicholas Hethe (*Reg. St Davids* 1 71–3; see above). Preb. of St Nicholas Penffoes 1405.

Richard Depedale ?–1398.

Vac. preb. before 14 Oct. 1398 (*Reg. St Davids* 1 89). Succeeded by Thomas Abbot (see below).

M. Thomas Abbot 1398–1400.

Coll. 14 Oct. 1398 to preb. vac. by Richard Depedale (*Reg. St Davids* 1 89; see above). D. before 7 Sept. 1400 (*Reg. St Davids* 1 179, 183). Succeeded by William Styuecle (see below).

M. William Styuecle B.C.L. 1400–1407.

Coll. 12 Sept. 1400 to preb. vac. by Thomas Abbot (*Reg. St Davids* 1 183; see above). D. before 10 Oct. 1407 (*CPR. 1405–1408* p. 371). Succeeded by John Gyles (see below p. 76).

M. John David 1402–1407.

Coll. 4 Aug. 1402 to preb. vac. by John Porter (*Reg. St Davids* 1 263; see above p. 74). D. before 21 Jan. 1407 (*Reg. St Davids* 1 379). Succeeded by John Colle (see below p. 76).

Thomas Tholite 1406–?

Mand. adm. 25 Jan. 1406 to preb. vac. by Richard Petir (*CPL.* VI 85; see above p. 74).

M. Robert Broun B.Th. ?–1406.

Exch. preb. with John Grandon for ch. of Chelsea, Mdx., 28 May 1406 (*Reg. St Davids* II 345; see below).

John Grandon 1406.

By exch. with Robert Broun for ch. of Chelsea, Mdx., 28 May 1406 (*Reg. St Davids* II 345; see above). Res. before 13 June (*Reg. St Davids* II 347). Succeeded by Robert Broun (see below p. 76).

[1] Philip Davy is said to have been adm. to the preb. vac. by John de Middleton in 1424 (*Menevia Sacra* p. 269—no reference given). This is said (*ibid.*) to have been the preb. of Llanddewi-Aberarth but there is insufficient evidence that Middleton held this. Middleton had royal gr. of the preb. vac. by John Sampson; John Sampson had been gr. the preb. vac. by Thomas Donclent, and all these people are listed as prebs. of Llanddewi-Aberarth in *Menevia Sacra*. The reference given is 'Reg. Cant.' (*ibid.* p. 268 n. 4). This reference must be Lamb., Reg. Courtenay f. 273b which records the admission 21 June 1389 of Sampson to the cursal preb. vac. by Thomas Donclent.

M. Robert Broun B.Th. 1406–?

Coll. 13 June 1406 to preb. vac. by John Grandon (*Reg. St Davids* II 347; see above p. 75).

M. John Colle Sch.C.L. 1407–?

Coll. 21 Jan. 1407 to preb. vac. by John David (*Reg. St Davids* I 379; see above p. 75).

M. John Gyles B.Th. 1407–?

Royal gr. 10 Oct. 1407 of preb. vac. by William Styuecle (*CPR. 1405–1408* p. 371; see above p. 75). Adm. 23 Nov. (*Reg. St Davids* II 407–9). ? Held preb. until d., c. Dec. 1428 (PCC 9 Luffenam).

Robert Burgeys 1408–?

Coll. 25 Jan. 1408 to preb. vac. by Thomas Guldesfeld (Reg. Hiot f. 2—in *Menevia Sacra* p. 304; see above p. 75).

Roger atte Herne 1413–?

Coll. 1 May 1413 to preb. vac. by Thomas Ayleward (Reg. Chichele f. 12—in *Menevia Sacra* p. 287; see above p. 75). Occ. 5 Sept. 1425 (*CPL.* VII 386–7).

Thomas Yonge 1415–1433.

Coll. 1415 (*Reg. Patrington* p. 41). Res. before 22 Aug. 1433 (*CPR. 1429–1436* p. 288). Succeeded by Thomas Rodburn (see below p. 77).

Richard Petir ?–1420.

D. as preb. before 26 Oct. 1420 (Reg. Nicholls f. 32b—in *Menevia Sacra* p. 293). Succeeded by Thomas Staundon (see below).

Thomas Staundon 1420–?

Coll. 26 Oct. 1420 to preb. vac. by Richard Petir (Reg. Nicholls f. 32b—in *Menevia Sacra* p. 293; see above).

M. Alexander Sparwe *or* **Herbard** B.Cn. & C.L. ?–1426.

Occ. 20 June 1421 (*CPL.* VII 176). Exch. preb. with John Brynk for free chap. of Membury, Devon, 8/9 July 1426 (Reg. Nicholls f. 49b—in *Menevia Sacra* p. 294; Salis., Reg. Chaundeler pt. i f. 91b; see below p. 77).

Richard Wogan ?–1426.

Exch. preb. with Dafydd ap Rhys for chancellorship 26 March 1426 (Reg. Nicholls f. 47b—in *Menevia Sacra* p. 144; see below).

M. Dafydd ap Rhys D.C.L. 1426–1431.

By exch. with Richard Wogan for chancellorship 26 March 1426 (Reg. Nicholls f. 47b—in *Menevia Sacra* p. 144; see above). Exch. cursal preb. and preb. of Clifton, Lincoln, with John Carpenter for preb. of Mathry, 7 Sept. 1431 (Reg. Nicholls f. 75—in *Menevia Sacra* p. 299; see below p. 77).

M. John Carpenter B.Th. ?–1426.

Res. preb. before 8 June 1426 when preb. of Mathry (Reg. Nicholls f. 48b—in *Menevia Sacra* p. 287). Succeeded by William Pirrye (see below).

William Pirrye 1426–?

Coll. 8 June 1426 to preb. vac. by John Carpenter (Reg. Nicholls f. 48b—in *Menevia Sacra* p. 287; see above).

Edmund Nicholls ?–1426.

Res. preb. before 8 June 1426 (Reg. Nicholls f. 48—in *Menevia Sacra* p. 309).

John Carpenter 1426–?

Coll. 8 June 1426 (Reg. Nicholls f. 48—in *Menevia Sacra* p. 309).[1]

M. John Brynk *or* **Dobeler** B.C.L. 1426–1447.

By exch. with Alexander Sparwe for free chap. of Membury, Devon, 8/9 July 1426 (Reg. Nicholls f. 49b—in *Menevia Sacra* p. 294; Salis., Reg. Chaundeler pt. i f. 91b; see above p. 76). Res. before 17 Aug. 1447 (Lamb., Reg. Stafford f. 95). Succeeded by Richard Owain (see below p. 78).

Thomas Bateman ?–1427.

Res. preb. before 17 March 1427 (Reg. Nicholls f. 57b—in *Menevia Sacra* p. 305). Succeeded by John Flore (see below).

John Flore 1427–?

Coll. 17 March 1427 to preb. vac. by Thomas Bateman (Reg. Nicholls f. 57b—in *Menevia Sacra* p. 305; see above).

M. Alexander Sparwe *or* **Herbard** B.Cn. & C.L. 1429.

Occ. 4 June 1429 (*CPL.* VIII 139–40). ? Held preb. until d., by Oct. 1433 (Salis., Reg. Neville pt. i f. 41b).

M. John Carpenter D.Th. 1431–1437.

By exch. with Dafydd ap Rhys for preb. of Mathry 7 Sept. 1431 (Reg. Nicholls f. 75—in *Menevia Sacra* p. 237; see above p. 76). Res. before 1 Apr. 1437 (Reg. Rodburn f. 125—in *Menevia Sacra* p. 299). Succeeded by Robert Montgomery (see below p. 78).

M. Thomas Rodburn Lic.Th. 1433.

Royal gr. 22 Aug. 1433 of preb. vac. by Thomas Yonge (*CPR. 1429–1436* p. 288; see above p. 76). Bp. of St Davids in Oct.

William Thame ?–1434.

Res. preb. before 30 June 1434 (Reg. Rodburn f. 103—in *Menevia Sacra* p. 305). Succeeded by Richard Newport (see below).

Richard Newport 1434–1436.

Coll. 30 June 1434 to preb. vac. by William Thame (Reg. Rodburn f. 103—in *Menevia Sacra* p. 305; see above). D. before 20 Aug. 1436 (Reg. Rodburn f. 121—in *Menevia Sacra* p. 305). Succeeded by John Burdet (see below p. 78).

William Rose ?–1435.

Vac. preb. at end of 1435 (Reg. Rodburn f. 117—in *Menevia Sacra* p. 287). Succeeded by John Waldebeff (see below).

John Waldebeff 1435–?

Adm. at end of 1435 to preb. vac. by William Rose (Reg. Rodburn f. 117—in *Menevia Sacra* p. 287; see above). ? Held preb. until 1452 when archdcn. of Brecon.

Thomas Yonge ?–1436.

D. as preb. before 20 July 1436 (Reg. Rodburn f. 120b—in *Menevia Sacra* p. 288). Succeeded by John Schipton (see below).

M. John Schipton 1436–1437.

Coll. 20 July 1436 to preb. vac. by Thomas Yonge (Reg. Rodburn f. 120b—in *Menevia Sacra* p. 288; see above). Exch. preb. with Roger de Bottal for treasurership 4 March 1437 (Reg. Rodburn f. 106—in *Menevia Sacra* pp. 160, 288; see below p. 78).

---

[1] Nicholls is said to have been probably succeeded by Carpenter (*Menevia Sacra* p. 309), but no definite reason is given for this statement. It is said that Carpenter is not to be identified with John Carpenter who held the preb. of Mathry and two other cursal prebs. in St Davids (*ibid.*).

M. John Burdet B.C.L. 1436–?
Coll. 20 Aug. 1436 to preb. vac. by Richard Newport (Reg. Rodburn f. 121—in *Menevia Sacra* p. 305; see above p. 77).

Roger de Bottal 1437–1439.
By exch. with John Schipton for treasurership 4 March 1437 (Reg. Rodburn f. 106 —in *Menevia Sacra* pp. 160, 288; see above p. 77). D. before 22 Oct. 1439 (Reg. Rodburn f. 111—in *Menevia Sacra* p. 288). Succeeded by William Fallan (see below).

Robert Montgomery 1437–1438.
Coll. 1 Apr. 1437 to preb. vac. by John Carpenter (Reg. Rodburn f. 125—in *Menevia Sacra* p. 299; see above p. 77). Res. before 28 Feb. 1438 (Reg. Rodburn f. 126—in *Menevia Sacra* p. 299). Succeeded by Richard Caunton (see below).

John Major ?–1437.
Res. preb. before 12 Apr. 1437[1] (Reg. Rodburn f. 126—in *Menevia Sacra* p. 309).

M. Richard Caunton D.C.L. 1438–?
Coll. 28 Feb. 1438 to preb. vac. by Robert Montgomery (Reg. Rodburn f. 126—in *Menevia Sacra* p. 299; see above).

William Fallan 1439–1446.
Coll. 22 Oct. 1439 to preb. vac. by Roger de Bottal (Reg. Rodburn f. 111—in *Menevia Sacra* p. 288; see above). Res. before 10 Nov. 1446 (*CPR. 1446–1452* p. 21). Succeeded by John Langton (see below).

M. John Langton Lic.Cn.L. 1446–1447.
Royal gr. 10 Nov. 1446 of preb. vac. by William Fallan (*CPR. 1446–1452* p. 21; see above). Bp. of St Davids 1447.

M. Richard Owain Sch.Th. 1447–?
Adm. 17 Aug. 1447 after royal gr. to preb. vac. by John Brynk (Lamb., Reg. Stafford f. 95; see above p. 77). ? Held preb. until d., before 2 June 1464 (PCC 7 Godyn).

M. Richard Andrew D.C.L. ?–1453.
Exch. preb. with William Hermer for a preb. in St George's chap., Windsor, Berks., 18 Dec. 1453 (*CPR. 1452–1461* p. 143; see below).

William Hermer 1453–?
By exch. with Richard Andrew for a preb. in St George's chap., Windsor, Berks., 18 Dec. 1453 (*CPR. 1452–1461* p. 143; see above).

M. Henry Pantry 1465.
Occ. 5 June 1465 (Worcester, Reg. Carpenter 1 f. 165).

M. Dafydd Williams D.Cn.L. ?–1482.
Res. preb. before 9 Aug. 1482 when archdcn. of St Davids (*Reg. St Davids* II 451). Succeeded by John Hunden[2] (see below).

M. John Hunden O.P., D.Th. 1482–?
Coll. 9 Aug. 1482 to preb. vac. by Dafydd Williams[2] (*Reg. St Davids* II 451; see above).

---

[1] 'Who his immediate successor was, is uncertain' (*Menevia Sacra* p. 309).
[2] Williams and Hunden appear to have exch. their benefices, the archdcnry of St Davids and a cursal preb., but there is no account of any negotiations for this exch. (see p. 60).

M. **William Eliot** B.C.L. ?–1487.
Res. preb. before 4 May 1487 when preb. of Trefloden (*Reg. St Davids* II 499). Succeeded by Richard Hill (see below).

M. **Richard Hill** B.Cn.L. 1487.
Coll. 4 May 1487 to preb. vac. by William Eliot (*Reg. St Davids* II 499; see above). Vac. preb. before 29 Aug. (*Reg. St Davids* II 505). Succeeded by Sampson (see below).

M. **Sampson** 1487–?
Coll. 29 Aug. 1487 to preb. vac. by Richard Hill (*Reg. St Davids* II 505; see above).

M. **Dafydd Wogan** B.Cn.L. 1487, 1504.
Occ. 13 Sept. 1487 (*Reg. St Davids* II 511). Occ. 8 July 1504 (Lamb., Reg. Warham II f. 223).

William Jonys 1501.
Occ. 16 Apr. 1501 (Brit. Mus., Harley MS. 1249 f. 273).

David O.Prem. Abbot of Talley. 1504.
Occ. 8 July 1504 (Lamb., Reg. Warham II f. 227).

M. **William Eliot** B.C.L. 1504.
Occ. 8 July 1504 (Lamb., Reg. Warham II f. 227). ? Held preb. until d., before 19 March 1507 (PCC 21 Adeane).

William Foxall 1504.
Occ. 8 July 1504 (Lamb., Reg. Warham II f. 227).

David Webbe 1504.
Occ. 8 July 1504 (Lamb., Reg. Warham II f. 227).

John Barlow 1539.
Occ. 1 Aug. 1539 (Nat. Libr. Wales, SD/Ch.B/1 p. 26).

Dafydd ap Hywel 1539, 1541.
Occ. 1 Aug. 1539, 1 Aug. 1541 (Nat. Libr. Wales, SD Ch.B/1 pp. 26, 28).

John ap Harry 1539, 1541.
Occ. 1 Aug. 1539, 1 Aug. 1541 (Nat. Libr. Wales, SD Ch.B/1 pp. 26, 28).

David Oliver 1539, 1541.
Occ. 1 Aug. 1539, 1 Aug. 1541 (Nat. Libr. Wales, SD Ch.B/1 pp. 26, 28).

Edward Pirson 1539, 1541.
Occ. 1 Aug. 1539, 1 Aug. 1541 (Nat. Libr. Wales, SD Ch.B/1 pp. 26, 28).

Morgan Lewis 1541.
Occ. 1 Aug. 1541 (Nat. Libr. Wales, SD Ch.B/1 p. 28). ? Held preb. until d., before 25 July 1554 (Nat. Libr. Wales, SD/BR/2 f. 6).

UNIDENTIFIED PREBENDARIES

M. **William Brunel** 1289, 1303.
Occ. 20 Nov. 1289 (*CPL.* I 506). Occ. 8 March 1303 (*ibid.* p. 609). Probably held preb. until d., Nov. 1304 (*Emden, Reg. Ox.* I 316).

John de Dalileye 1306, 1307.
Occ. as can. 22 March 1306 (*CPL.* II 21). Occ. as preb. 5 Feb. 1307 (*ibid.* p. 37).

John de Drokensford ?–1309.
Occ. 1 March 1308 (*CPL*. II 39). Bp. of Bath and Wells 1309.

M. Philip de Turvil 1309, 1328.
Occ. 9 Aug. 1309 (Worcester, Reg. Sede Vacante f. 69b). Occ. 21 Apr. 1328 (Cant., Reg. Q f. 166b).

Ingelard de Warley 1310.
Occ. 1 May 1310 (*CPL*. II 72).

Walter de Pederton 1311.
Occ. 14 Feb. 1311 (*CPL*. II 81).

M. Roger de Northburgh 1317.
Occ. 14 March 1317 (*CPL*. II 143). ? Held preb. until bp. of Coventry and Lichfield, el. 1321, cons. 1322.

M. James de Berkeley M.A. 1317, 1318.
Occ. 19 March 1317 and 28 July 1318 (*CPL*. II 149, 174).

M. Walter Alexander 1317–1349.
Prov. to canonry with reservn. of preb. 19 March 1317 (*CPL*. II 143). Occ. as can. 26 July 1339 (Brit. Mus., Harley MS. 6280 f. 58b). D. as preb. before 14 June 1349 (*CPP*. I 169). Succeeded by David Martin of Rosemarket (see below p. 81).

John de Depyng 1322.
Occ. 21 Jan. 1322 (*CPL*. II 225).

Rhys ap Hywel ?–1328.
Occ. 11 Apr. 1328 (Cant., Reg. Q f. 166b). Vac. preb. before 22 May (*CPR*. *1327–1330* p. 273). Succeeded by John de Camera (see below).

M. John Walwayn D.C.L. ?–1330.
Occ. as can. 21 Apr. 1328 (Cant., Reg. Q f. 163). Occ. as preb. 13 June 1330 (*CPL*. II 315). D. before 9 Dec. (Lincoln, Reg. IV (Burghersh) f. 73b). Succeeded by John Cok and Richard de Turville (see below).

M. Nigel de Wavere Lic.Th. 1328, 1330.
Occ. as can. 11 May 1328 (Cant., Reg. Q f. 166b). Occ. as preb. 5 June 1330 (*CPL*. II 324).

John de Camera 1328–?
Royal gr. 22 May 1328 of preb. vac. by Rhys ap Hywel (*CPR*. *1327–1330* p. 273; see above). Occ. 10 July 1329 (*CPL*. II 294).

Walter de Salopia 1328–?
Prov. 4 July 1328 (*CPL*. II 275).

M. Stephen de Ketelbiri D.C.L. 1343–?
Prov. 19 Feb. 1343 (*CPP*. I 13).

John Cok 1345–?
M. Richard de Turville Sch.Th. 1345–1361.
Cok prov. 14 Sept. 1345 to preb. vac. by John Walwayn (*CPP*. I 84; see above). Prov. again 2 Oct. because preb. already occupied by Turville (*CPP*. I 86). Turville petitioned 7 Aug. 1346 for conf. of coll. to preb. by bp. (*ibid*. p. 115). Cok evidently res. preb. because occ. 11 May 1349 as can. with reservn. of preb. in St Davids (*ibid*. p. 158). Turville vac. preb. before 7 Sept. 1361 (*CPR*. *1361–1364* p. 58). Succeeded by Richard Carru (see below p. 81).

M. Adam de Houghton D.C.L. ?–1356.

Occ. 1 Feb. 1347 and 8 May 1350 (*CPL.* III 258, 336). Preb. of Mathry 1356.

M. Richard Fychan D.C.L. 1347–1352.

Prov. to canonry with reservn. of preb. 21 Apr. 1347 (*CPL.* III 220). Vac. preb. before 21 July 1352 (*CPR. 1350–1354* p. 306). Succeeded by Walter de Leghton (see below).

William Laci 1347–?

Prov. 23 Nov. 1347 (*CPP.* I 124).

M. David Martin of Rosemarket B.C.L. 1349–1361.

Prov. 14 June 1349 to preb. vac. by Walter Alexander (*CPP.* I 169; see above p. 80). Vac. preb. before 16 July 1361 (*CPR. 1361–1364* p. 40). Succeeded by John de Saxton (see below).

M. Reginald Brian Lic.C.L. ?–1349.

Vac. preb. 1349 when bp. of St Davids (*CPL.* III 316). Succeeded by John Sais (see below).

John Sais 1349–?

Prov. 18 Oct. 1349 to preb. vac. by Reginald Brian (*CPL.* III 316; see above). Occ. 15 Oct. 1366 (*Reg. Langham* pp. 23–4).

John de Brian 1351.

Occ. as can. 31 Aug. 1351 (*CPL.* II 445). Vac. preb. n.d., succeeded by Philip de Brian (Salis., Reg. Erghum f. 59; see below p. 82).

Walter de Leghton 1352.

Estate ratif. 21 July 1352 in preb. vac. by Richard Fychan (*CPR. 1350–1354* p. 306; see above).

Walter de Elisaundre ?–1353.

Vac. preb. before 28 May 1353 (*CPR. 1350–1354* p. 445). Succeeded by Robert Burbach (see below).

Robert Burbach 1353–?

Royal gr. 28 May 1353 of preb. vac. by Walter de Elisaundre (*CPR. 1350–1354* p. 445; see above).

M. Robert de Middelond D.Th. 1358–?

Prov. to canonry with reservn. of preb. 20 March 1358 (*CPL.* II 592). Occ. as preb. 19 Dec. 1365 (*CPP.* I 510).

John de Saxton 1361.

Royal gr. 16 July 1361 of preb. vac. by David Martin of Rosemarket (*CPR. 1361–1364* p. 40; see above). Preb. of Caerfai 30 July.

Richard Carru 1361–?

Royal gr. 7 Sept. 1361 of preb. vac. by Richard de Turville (*CPR. 1361–1364* p. 58; see above p. 80).

M. Richard Cleangre D.Th. ?–1361.

Vac. preb. before 22 Nov. 1361 (*CPR. 1361–1364* p. 117). Succeeded by William de Wykeham (see below).

William de Wykeham 1361–1362.

Royal gr. 22 Nov. 1361 of preb. vac. by Richard Cleangre (*CPR. 1361–1364* p. 117; see above). Exch. preb. with William de Burghbrigg for preb. of Crowhurst, Hastings royal free chap., Suss., 15 Feb. 1362 (*CPR. 1361–1364* pp. 167–8; see below p. 82).

Thomas Bluet ?–1362.

D. as preb. before 14 Jan. 1362 (*CPR. 1361–1364* p. .138). Succeeded by John de Swynlegh (see below).

John de Swynlegh 1362–?

Royal gr. 14 Jan. 1362 of preb. vac. by Thomas Bluet (*CPR. 1361–1364* p. 138; see above).

William de Burghbrigg 1362–?

By exch. with William de Wykeham for preb. of Crowhurst, Hastings royal free chap., 15 Feb. 1362 (*CPR. 1361–1364* pp. 167–8; see above p. 81). Occ. July 1366 (*Reg. Sudbury* II 171). ? Held preb. until d., before 31 Jan. 1392 (Salis., Reg. Waltham f. 200).

M. Ralph de Langley D.Th. 1363–?

Prov. to canonry with reservn. of preb. 22 Feb. 1363 (*CPP.* I 404). Occ. 24 Apr. (*ibid.* p. 441).

Robert de Witeberg 1363.

Occ. 22 Apr. 1363 (*CPP.* I 416).

Robert Mason 1366.

Occ. 8 Oct. 1366 (*Reg. Langham* p. 31).

John de Tuverton 1366.

Occ. 10 Oct. 1366 (*Reg. Langham* p. 79).

Philip de Brian ?–1381.

Exch. preb. vac. by John de Brian (see above p. 81) with Guy de Erle for free chap. of Stratford sub Castle, Wilts., 26 Nov. 1381 (Salis., Reg. Erghum f. 59; see below).

Guy de Erle 1381–?

By exch. with Philip de Brian for free chap. of Stratford sub Castle, Wilts., 26 Nov. 1381 (Salis., Reg. Erghum f. 59; see above).

Richard de Caunton ?–1390.

Res. preb. before 21 Feb. 1390 because had appropriated it to archdcnry of Cardigan without royal lic. (*CPR. 1388–1392* p. 198). Succeeded by John Prata (see below).

John Prata 1390–?

Royal gr. 21 Feb. 1390 to preb. vac. by Richard de Caunton (*CPR. 1388–1392* p. 198; see above).

M. John Trefor D.Cn. & C.L. 1390–1394.

Prov. to canonry with reservn. of preb. 9 Nov. 1390 (*CPL.* IV 343). Vac. preb. 1394 when bp. of St Asaph (*ibid.* p. 475). Succeeded by Richard Possewyk of Avignon (see below).

John Bodeln 1390.

Occ. 7 Dec. 1390 (*CPL.* IV 399).

Richard Possewyk of Avignon 1394–?

Prov. 25 Nov. 1394 to preb. vac. by John Trefor (*CPL.* IV 475; see above). Occ. 15 Aug. 1402 (*CPL.* IV 576).

Henry Nahim ?–1398.

Exch. preb. with Dafydd Gwyn for ch. of Llanarth, Card., 27 Oct. 1398 (*Reg. St Davids* I 89; see below p. 83).

Dafydd Gwyn 1398–?

By exch. with Henry Nahim for ch. of Llanarth, Card., 27 Oct. 1398 (*Reg. St Davids* I 89; see above p. 82).

M. Thomas Abbot ?–1400.

D. as preb. before 7 Sept. 1400 (*Reg. St Davids* I 179). Succeeded by Richard Leyntwardyn (see below).

Richard Leyntwardyn 1400–1406.

Coll. 7 Sept. 1400 to preb. vac. by Thomas Abbot (*Reg. St Davids* I 179; see above). Res. before 24 March 1406 (*Reg. St Davids* I 339). Succeeded by Philip Craddock (see below).

M. Philip Craddock 1406–?

Coll. 24 March 1406 to preb. vac. by Richard Leyntwardyn (*Reg. St Davids* I 339; see above).

M. Roger Basset D.Cn. & C.L. ?–1416.

D. as preb.[1] 16/26 Sept. 1416 (PCC 35 Marche).

Thomas Faukes 1431.

Occ. 17 Apr. 1431 (*CPL.* VIII 323).

M. John Smith D.Th. 1476.

Held preb. in St Davids when prov. to bpc. of Llandaff c. March 1476 (*CPL.* XIII ii 480). Gr. lic. to retain preb. *in commendam* with bpc. (*ibid.*).

David Stedman 1502.

Held prebendal stall in cath. 24 Sept. 1502 (*Reg. St Davids* II 743).

CANONS WITH EXPECTATION OF PREBENDS

John de Baskerville 1320–?
Prov. 14 Jan. 1320 (*CPL.* II 195). Occ. 28 Apr. 1328 (Cant., Reg. Q f. 163).

Walter de Barwe 1323–?
Prov. 23 July 1323 (*CPL.* II 232).

Richard de Hoo 1327–?
Prov. 17 July 1327 (*CPL.* II 259). Occ. 11 Aug. 1331 (*ibid.* p. 345).

John de Frechvill 1329–?
Prov. 14 Sept. 1329 (*CPL.* II 308).

Geoffrey de Bikeleswade 1331–?
Prov. 23 June 1331 (*CPL.* II 344).

M. Thomas de Aschele B.C.L. 1332–?
Prov. 24 Jan. 1332 (*CPL.* II 355).

John de Bodringham 1344–?
Prov. 24 Aug. 1344 (*CPL.* III 102).

John de Boys 1345–?
Prov. 25 March 1345 (*CPL.* III 151).

Richard de Haningfelde 1348–?
Prov. 19 May 1348 (*CPP.* I 162).

---

[1] This preb. was possibly the preb. of Llandyssilio-gogo which Basset held as treasurer.

John Cok 1349.
Occ. 11 May 1349 (*CPP.* I 158).

M. Llywellyn de Brechonia B.Cn.L. 1363–?
Prov. 10 June 1363 (*CPP.* I 426). Occ. 22 Aug. (*ibid.* p. 452).

M. Robert de Thorp M.A. 1363–?
Prov. 26 June 1363 (*CPP.* I 436).

Hugh Bridham 1363–?
Prov. Aug. 1363 (*CPP.* I 445).

Philip Martin 1363–?
Prov. 31 Oct. 1363 (*CPL.* III 480).

M. John Skyret of Buckingham B.C.L. 1364–?
Prov. Apr. 1364 (*CPP.* I 488). Occ. 4 May 1366 (*CPL.* IV 55–6).

Thomas Karlelle 1393–?
Prov. 28 Oct. 1393 (*CPL.* IV 467).

M. Griffin le Yonge D.Cn.L. 1401.
Gr. royal pardon 20 Dec. 1401 for accepting prov. (*CPR. 1401–1405* p. 30).

CANONS OF ST DAVIDS

M. John Bouhs 1307, 1317.
Occ. 1307 (*Reg. Corbridge* II 167 n. 1). Occ. 1 Apr. 1317 (*CPL.* II 145).

M. Henry de Gower 1314.
Occ. 1314 (*Foedera* II iv 360).

M. Peter de Berkeley 1320–?
Prov. 17 June 1320 (*CPL.* II 204). Occ. 21 Apr. 1328 (Cant., Reg. Q f. 166b).
? Held canonry until d., before Apr. 1342 (Salis., Reg. Wyville II ii f. 103).

Hugh de Welhampton 1328.
Occ. 21 Apr. 1328 (Cant., Reg. Q f. 166b).

Thomas Rose 1328.
Occ. 11 May 1328 (Cant., Reg. Q f. 161b).

M. William de Carrewe 1328.
Occ. 21 May 1328 (Cant., Reg. Q f. 166).

Thomas Fleming 1328.
Occ. 21 May 1328 (Cant., Reg. Q f. 166).

Walter de Hulle 1328, 1342.
Occ. 21 May 1328 (Cant., Reg. Q f. 166). Occ. 27 May 1342 (Brit. Mus., Harley
MS. 6280 f. 15).

John de Lynham 1328, 1333.
Occ. 21 May 1328 (Cant., Reg. Q f. 166). Occ. 26 July 1333 (Brit. Mus., Harley
MS. 6280 f. 57b).

William Mey 1335, 1339.
Occ. 14 Feb. 1335 (Brit. Mus., Harley MS. 6280 f. 59b). Occ. 26 July 1339 (*ibid.*
f. 57b).

John Carman 1339.
Occ. 26 July 1339 (Brit. Mus., Harley MS. 6280 f. 57b).

M. Simon de Witton 1339, 1342.
Occ. 26 July 1339 (Brit. Mus., Harley MS. 6280 f. 57b). Occ. 27 May 1342 (*ibid.* f. 15).

John Goch 1348, 1349.
Occ. 1 May 1348 (*CPL.* III 246). Occ. 27 Aug. 1349 (*ibid.* p. 345).

Richard de Thoresby 1349.
Occ. 24 Dec. 1349 (*CPL.* III 321).

Morgan ab Einion 1391.
Occ. 16 Jan. 1391 (*CPL.* IV 416). ? Held canonry until d., before 21 Apr. 1408 (*CPR. 1405–1408* p. 423).

John Hyot[1] 1420.
Occ. 18 March 1420 (*CPL.* VII 341).

M. Philip David ?–1425.
D. as can. before 5 Jan. 1425 (*Reg. Chichele* II 304).

M. John Flour B.Cn. & C.L. 1441.
Occ. 10 March 1441 (*CPL.* IX 233).[2]

M. Richard Caunton D.C.L. 1445, 1459.[3]
Occ. 24 Dec. 1445 (*CPL.* VIII 305). Occ. 18 July 1459 (*ibid.* XI 548).

Ralph Dreff 1446.
Occ. 8 Nov. 1446 (P.R.O., C 84/46/41).

Huw Pavy 1446.
Occ. 8 Nov. 1446 (P.R.O., C 84/46/41).

M. Lewis Owain ab Owain D.Cn.L. 1466.
Occ. 30 Aug. 1466 (*CPL.* XII 587).

John William 1476.
Occ. 9 Feb. 1476 (*CPL.* XIII ii 496).

Thomas O.Can.S.A. Prior of Carmarthen. 1493.
Adm. 3 March 1493 (*Reg. St Davids* II 647). Promised s.d. the next cursal preb. to become vac. (*ibid.*).

[1] Hyot can possibly be identified with M. John Hiot archdcn. of St Davids, d. before 31 May 1420 (see p. 60). As archdcn. he would have held the preb. of Mydrim and as the terms canon and prebendary seem often to have been used interchangeably, he could have been described as 'canon of St Davids' in 1420 instead of his full title 'archdcn. of St Davids and preb. of Mydrim'. However, the John Hyot above does not occur with the title *Magister* and it seems improbable that this would have been omitted for M. John Hiot who had been custodian of St Davids diocese, *sede vacante*, after bp. Mona's death in 1407 and vicar general of bp. Chichele and was evidently an important person. John Hyot above has therefore been considered a separate person, perhaps a member of the same family named after his illustrious relative.
[2] John Flour can probably be identified with John Flore who was coll. to a cursal preb. 1427 (see p. 77) but as the evidence is insufficient for this identification the names have been given separately.
[3] The term 'canon' appears to have been used in a general sense here. Caunton held a cursal preb. 1438; in 1446 he was archdcn. of Cardigan and would have held the preb. of Llandyfriog; he was chancellor in 1453 and would have held the preb. of Llawhaden, and in 1459 he occ. as archdcn. of St Davids and would have held the preb. of Mydrim. In spite of all his offices he is simply described by the clerks of the curia as a canon 1445 and 1459. He has been listed here among the canons, although in 1445 the title 'cursal prebendary' was probably intended and in 1459 'prebendary of Mydrim'.

APPENDIX

Note on the order of the dignitaries

Comparatively few Welsh dignitaries have been found for the period 1300–1541 and the history of the composition of the four cathedral chapters is relatively obscure. The Welsh sees were extremely poor and 'in terms of English bishoprics they were all indecently unrewarding' (*Williams* p. 270). The Welsh cathedral benefices were evidently of even less comparative monetary value than the bishoprics[1] and it seems that in most cases there was virtually no difference in seniority. In the cathedrals of Bangor and St Asaph where the traditional four dignitaries, dean, chancellor, precentor and treasurer are found, these have been listed simply in alphabetical order following the deans. In Llandaff there was no office of dean until the nineteenth century and his place as head of the chapter was filled by the archdeacon of Llandaff,[2] who in this case took precedence over the other dignitaries. The archdeacons of Llandaff have therefore been listed after the bishops, and are followed by the chancellors, precentors and treasurers. In St Davids there was similarly no office of dean until the nineteenth century[3] and his position as head of the chapter was held by the precentor. The precentors of St Davids have been listed immediately after the bishops, and are followed by the chancellors and treasurers. The archdeacons, with the exception of the archdeacon of Llandaff, are given after the cathedral dignitaries. In Bangor and St Davids the archdeacons of the cathedral cities took precedence over the others as was usual in other dioceses. There was only one archdeacon in St Asaph diocese until the nineteenth century when the archdeaconry of Montgomery was created.[4]

In the four dioceses the prebends have been arranged in alphabetical order and the unidentified prebendaries in order of their collation or first occurrence. The six cursal prebends of St Davids have also been arranged in the above chronological sequence (see p. 73) as no evidence has been found to show that they were ever distinguished by name or number. The grouping of these prebends by archdeacon Yardley (archdeacon of Cardigan 1739–1770) as 'Cursal prebend A. B. C. D. E. and F.' has for this reason been disregarded since it appears to have been an arbitrary arrangement, with much of the evidence for the succession of prebendaries resting on supposition. Yardley himself included a list of the prebendal stalls in St Davids cathedral (*Menevia*

---

[1] A detailed account is given of the incomes of the Welsh clergy in *Williams* pp. 269–95.

[2] The deanery of Llandaff was created by two Parliamentary Statutes 3 & 4 Victoria c. 113 and 6 & 7 Victoria c. 7. The first provides that the new office of dean should be held by the archdcn. of Llandaff, the traditional head of the cathedral chapter and the second that the two offices should be distinct and held by two different persons.

[3] *Williams* p. 315 n. 2.

[4] Between the years 1589 and 1843/4 the archdcnry of St Asaph was held *in commendam* with the bpc. This archdcnry was revived as a separate office by Statute 6 & 7 Victoria, 1843/4 and the archdcnry of Montgomery created by an Order in Council 31 Jan. 1844 as a second archdcnry (*Thomas* I 245).

Sacra pp. 18–19) and this shows that there was no distinguishing mark for these six cursal prebends: the names of the prebends are those given by Yardley.

South Side	North Side
Dominus Episcopus	Precentor
Archidiaconus Meneviensis	Archidiaconus Brecon
P. Landewy	P. S. Nicholai
P. Cursalis	P. Llangan
P. Treflydn	P. Cursalis
uninscribed stall	stall without title
Vicarius episcopalis	Succentor
P. Cursalis	P. Cursalis
P. Cursalis	P. Cursalis
P. Clydeu	P. Caerfai
uninscribed stall	stall without inscription
P. Caer Farchell	Archidiaconus Cardigan
Archidiaconus Carmarth'	P. Aurea [Mathry]
Cancellarius	Thesaurarius

Index

PERSONS

PLACES